ADAMS

TIME MANAGEMENT

D0815771

Business titles from Adams Media Corporation

Accounting for the New Business, by Christopher R. Malburg

Adams Businesses You Can Start Almanac

Adams Streetwise Complete Business Plan, by Bob Adams

Adams Streetwise Consulting, by David Kintler

Adams Streetwise Customer-Focused Selling, by Nancy Stephens

Adams Streetwise Do-It-Yourself Advertising, by Sarah White and John Woods

Adams Streetwise Hiring Top Performers, by Bob Adams and Peter Veruki

Adams Streetwise Managing People, by Bob Adams, et al.

Adams Streetwise Small Business Start-Up, by Bob Adams

All-in-One Business Planner, by Christopher R. Malburg

Buying Your Own Business, by Russell Robb

Entrepreneurial Growth Strategies, by Lawrence W. Tuller

Exporting, Importing, and Beyond, by Lawrence W. Tuller

How to Become Successfully Self-Employed, by Brian R. Smith

How to Start and Operate a Successful Home Business, by David E. Rye

Independent Consultant's Q&A Book, by Lawrence W. Tuller

Management Basics, by John & Shirley Payne

Managing People, by Darien McWhirter

Marketing Magic, by Don Debelak

New A-Z of Managing People, by David Freemantle

The Personnel Policy Handbook for Growing Companies, by Darien McWhirter

Presentations, by Daria Price Bowman

Selling 101: A Course for Business Owners and Non-Sales People,
by Michael T. McGaulley

Service, Service, Service: A Secret Weapon for Your Growing Business,
by Steve Albrecht

The Small Business Legal Kit, by J. W. Dicks

The Small Business Valuation Book, by Lawrence W. Tuller

Streetwise Business Forms, by Bob Adams

Streetwise Business Letters, by John Woods

Streetwise Motivating and Rewarding Employees, by Alexander Hiam

Streetwise Time Management, by Marshall J. Cook

Available through your favorite bookseller.

ADAMS

TIME MANAGEMENT

Proven Techniques for Making the Most of Your Valuable Time

MARSHALL J. COOK

Adams Media Corporation
Holbrook, Massachusetts

This is a *CWL Publishing Enterprises Book*, developed by John A. Woods
for Adams Media Corporation. For more information, contact CWL Publishing
Enterprises at 3010 Irvington Way, Madison, WI 53713-3414, (608) 273-3710.

Published by
Adams Media Corporation
260 Center Street, Holbrook, MA 02343

ISBN: 1-55850-799-X

Printed in the United States of America.

J   I   H   G   F   E   D   C

Library of Congress Cataloging-in-Publication Data
Cook, Marshall J.
    Time management : proven techniques for making the most of your
valuable time / Marshall J. Cook.
        p.   cm.
    Includes index.
    ISBN 1-55850-799-X
    1. Time Management. I. Title.
    HD69.T54C66   1998
    650.1—dc21   97-46962
                                                                  CIP

This publication is designed to provide accurate and authoritative information
with regard to the subject matter covered. It is sold with the understanding that
the publisher is not engaged in rendering legal, accounting, or other professional
advice. If legal advice or other expert assistance is required, the services of a
competent professional person should be sought.
    — From a *Declaration of Principles* jointly adopted by a Committee of the
American Bar Association and a Committee of Publishers and Associations

This book is available at quantity discounts for bulk purchases.
For information, call 1-800-872-5627 (in Massachusetts, 781-767-8100).

Visit our home page at http://www.adamsmedia.com

Contents

PREFACE xvii
ACKNOWLEDGMENTS xix

1. DO YOU HAVE SPEED SICKNESS?
Learn to Detect Adrenaline Addiction and Other
    Symptoms of the Madness 1
Riding the Adrenaline High 4
Simple Symptoms and Scary Consequences
    of Speed Sickness 5
Reports of the "Death of Work" Premature 6
We Have Seen the Enemy, and It Is Us 7
Just What *Is* Time, Anyway? 8

2. ARE YOU REALLY AS BUSY AS YOU THINK?
Find Out How You're Really Spending Your Time . . . 11
A Nation of Watchers and Shoppers? 12
How Are You "Spending" Your Life? 14

3. CAN YOU REALLY MANAGE TIME?
Learn What to Control and What to Let Go 19
Just What *Can* You Do about the Time Crunch? 20
Limits to the Traditional Time Management
    Approach 21
So That's Where the Time *Really* Goes! 24
Some Initial Changes to Get Control of Your Time . . 24

4. DO YOU RUN THE LIST, OR DOES THE LIST RUN YOU?

Learn to Use the To-Do List Effectively. 27
The To-Do List from Hell 28
The Day as You Really Live It 29
10 Suggestions for Creating a Healthy To-Do List . . 30
    1. Don't Put Too Much on It 30
    2. Put Some Air in It 31
    3. List Possibilities, Not Imperatives 31
    4. Don't Carve the List on Stone Tablets 33
    5. Order Creatively 33
    6. Break the Boulders into Pebbles. 33
    7. Schedule Breaks, Goofs, Time-Out Time, and
       Little Rewards 34
    8. Schedule for the Long Range as Well as
       Short-Term Goals 35
    9. Be Ready to Abandon the List 35
   10. You Don't Have to Make a List at All. 36
    Bonus Suggestions: Create a Not-To-Do List 36

5. GETTING STARTED:

Learn How to Jump-Start Each Work Session 37
Seven Ways to Get a Fast Start 37
    1. Prepare Mentally 37
    2. Prepare Physically 38
    3. Map the Terrain 39
    4. Start Anywhere 39
    5. Start Anyway 40
    6. Lock Out the Critics. 40
    7. Stop Before You Need To. 41

6. IS YOUR LIFE A CONSTANT TWO-MINUTE DRILL?

Learn How to Call Time Out—
and Put Power in the Pause 43

You Know You're Running Your Two-Minute
   Offense When 43
Warning: Major Metaphor Shift Here from the
   Football Field to the Surf........................ 44
Putting the Power in the Pause—
   Taking Mini-Vacations Every Day 45
Seven Ways to Go on Vacation Without
   Leaving Your Desk......................... 45
   1. The Breath Break....................... 45
   2. The Continental Drift.................... 46
   3. Pack Up Your Troubles................... 46
   4. The Shoulder Shrug..................... 47
   5. The Phrase for the Day 47
   6. The Object of Your Affection 47
   7. Advance Resting Technique 48
Why the Two-Minute Break Works.............. 48
Free 21-Day Satisfaction-Guaranteed Tension Trial. . 48

7. **IF YOU DON'T KNOW WHERE YOU'RE
   GOING, HOW WILL YOU KNOW WHEN
   YOU GET THERE?**
   Learn How to Get Organized 51
   Assessing Your Personal Style.................. 53
   How to See the Forest *and* the Trees............. 54
   Breaking Goals into Steps..................... 55
   Scheduling Those Steps 57
   Evaluation................................ 58

8. **IS IT REALLY IMPORTANT—OR MERELY
   URGENT?**
   Learn How to Create Order from the Daily Chaos . . 59
   The Dilemma of the Ringing Telephone 61
   Is It Important or Merely Urgent?............... 63
   The Four Categories of All Life's Activities 64

The Secret of Time Management Revealed:
Why We Waste Time on Trivia and Don't Spend
Enough Time on Essentials 66
Asking the "Want To/Have To" Question 67
Knowing When Time Isn't Really the Problem 68
Why You'll Never Be Able to "Find" Time 68

9. WHO'S SETTING YOUR AGENDA?
Learn How to Deal with the Time Snatchers 71
The Three Little Words That Can Steal Your Life . . . 71
What's Wrong with "Buzz Off"? 72
What about That Old Standby, "No"? 73
The Golden Rule Applied to the Three
Little Words 73
Recovering from the "Take a Meeting" Syndrome . . 74
It's Okay to Draw a Blank 75
Planning by the Colors Instead of the Numbers 76
Who Really Has a Claim on Your Time? 77
Should the Squeaky Wheel Get All Your Grease?. 77
When You Should Chuck Time Management:
A Morality Tale 78

10. IS YOUR STAFF WORKING EFFICIENTLY?
Seven Time Management Tips for Managers 81
1. Never Waste Their Time 81
2. Make Sure the Time Savers
Are Really Saving Their Time 82
3. Separate the Important from the Merely
Urgent for Your Staff 82
4. Tell Them Why 83
5. Allow Them Enough Time for the Task 83
6. Encourage Them to Do One Thing Well—
at a Time 83
7. Cut Down on Meeting Time! 83

11. DOES YOUR "NO" REALLY MEAN "NO"?

*Learn How to Avoid Taking on Everybody
Else's Burdens* 87
The Not-So-Nice Reasons for Being So Nice 88
   Why All That "Yes" Sneaks Up on You 89
He Ain't Heavy; He's My Colleague............. 90
A Qualitative Method for Computing
the True Cost of Your Commitments 90
Another Subjective Method for
Trimming the Activity List................... 92
The "Something's Got to Give"
Theory of Time Management................ 93
Heartless? Humbug! 94
How to Say "No" 95

12. ARE ALL YOUR GADGETS REALLY SAVING YOU TIME?

Learn How to Manage the Machines............. 97
Tallying the True Cost of Technology in Terms
of Time 98
   The Time It Takes to Select It 98
   The Time It Takes to Learn How to Use It 99
   The Time It Takes to Get It Fixed............ 100
   Downtime 100
Facing Up to the Annoyance Factor 101
Can You Retain "High Touch" in the
Age of Technology?...................... 101
The Paradox of "Impersonal Communication" 102
Technology as a Waste of Time................ 103
What Has Happened to All the Time
You've "Saved"? 103
Retaking Control of the Technology 105
   Three Ways to Make Good Decisions about
Technology........................... 106

13. DO YOU KNOW SO MUCH YOU DON'T KNOW ANYTHING?

Learn How to Combat Information Overload 109
Four Fundamental Truths about the Internet 111
   1. Most People Aren't on It Yet. 111
   2. The Net Won't Wipe Out Other Media 111
   3. You Won't Become a Net Junkie. 112
   4. Information Is Not Wisdom. 112
You Are the Quality Control 112
Five Ways to Verify Information on the Net 113
   1. Check the Date 113
   2. Consider the Source 113
   3. Track Down the Ultimate Source 113
   4. Separate Fact Statements from Opinion
      Statements 114
   5. Cross-Check. 115
Three Ways to Avoid Drowning in
All That Information 115
   1. Give Yourself Permission Not to Know
      Everything about Everything. 115
   2. Rip, Read, and Recycle. 115
   3. Create a Reading File for Airports, Busses,
      and Waiting Rooms. 116
Mark Your Sources and Stick with Them 116
An Ode to the Joys of Aimless Browsing 118

14. SPEED WRITING:

*Learn How to Get It Down on Paper or
Up on the Screen ASAP* 119
Five Tips for Writing It Right—and Fast—
the First Time. 119
   1. Keep It Short and Simple 119
   2. Get Off to a Flying Start 120
   3. Sustain the Flow 121
   4. Finish Cleanly 122
   5. Edit by the Numbers 122

A Cautionary Note about Editing 123
The Pros and Cons of Instant Writing 123

15. DROWNING IN A SEA OF PAPER?
Learn How to Control the Flood 125
10 Ways You Can Reduce, Control, and
    Eliminate Paper 125
   1. Adopt a Constant Companion 125
   2. Manage Your Desktop(s) 126
   3. Touch It Once 126
   4. Exercise Good Sortsmanship 127
   5. Make It Disappear 127
   6. RSVP ASAP 127
   7. File It and Forget It? 128
   8. Strip, Clip, and Flip 128
   9. Shift Gears When You Read 128
  10. The Cop-Out Compost Heap 129

16. HOW LONG SINCE YOU'VE SEEN YOUR DESK?
Learn How to Cut Through the Clutter 131
Clutter Question #1: Can You Find It? 131
Clutter Question #2: Are You Comfortable with
    Things the Way They Are? 132
Impractical Solution #1: Let Somebody Else
    Cull the Paper 132
Impractical Solution #2: Train Your Sources to
    Limit the Paper 133
Why Do We Make the Mess? 133
   1. The Nesting Instinct 134
   2. Saver Spillover 134
   3. Out of Sight, Out of Mind 135
   4. The Einstein Complex 135
Small Steps, Big Strides 135
Ongoing Maintenance 137
Incoming! 137

17. TIRED OF WAITING?
*Learn How to Turn Downtime into Your
  Most Productive Time* 141
Why Don't Adults Get Bored? 142
One Bad Way to Do Away with Waiting 143
One Okay Way to Eliminate Some of the Waiting... 144
You Might Be Able to Make the Wait Matter Less .. 144
You'll *Always* Have to Wait.................. 144
How to Use the Wait Time: Three Steps
  That Will Make You More Productive *and*
  Less Rushed............................ 145
  Step 1. Accept the Wait as Inevitable 145
  Step 2. Rename the Wait 146
  Step 3. *Use* the Wait.................... 146
Results of Turning the Wait into a Rest 147

18. ARE YOU PAYING A HIGH PRICE FOR PROCRASTINATION?
Learn How to Put Off the Urge to Put It Off 149
Five Reasons Why We Procrastinate and
  Five Strategies to Put Off Putting Off. 150
  Reason 1. You Haven't Really Committed to
    Doing the Job 150
  Reason 2. You're Afraid of the Job........... 152
  Reason 3. You Don't Place a High Enough
    Priority on the Activity 153
  Reason 4. You Don't Know Enough to
    Do the Task.......................... 154
  Reason 5. You Just Plain Don't Wanna! 155

19. JUST *DON'T* DO IT!
*Learn How to Get Rid of the Tasks
  You Don't Want or Need to Do*............... 157
How to Eliminate Unnecessary Steps 157
  Get Rid of the Cobweb Catacombs 157

Two More Forms of Unnecessary Work—
   Busy Work and Work Avoidance Work 159
The *"Not-*To-Do" List and the "Let Others Do It" List . . 160
Delegating, Swapping, and Letting Go 161
   1. Delegating 161
   2. Swapping 162
   3. Letting Go 162
Do It Now, Do It Later, or Do It Never 162
Peeling Off the Layers of Perfection: The "Good
   Enough" Tenet of Time Management 163

20. WHOSE DRUM DO YOU MARCH TO?
Learn to Keep Time to Your Own (Bio)rhythms 165
What Would You Do if You Could Do
   Whatever You Wanted To? 166
So, What Can You Do about It? 167
How to Find Your Rhythm 168
   1. Establish a Fairly Regular Pattern 170
   2. Eat When You're Hungry, Not When It's Time . . 170
   3. Take Your Nourishment in Smaller Portions . 170
   4. Nap. 171
   5. Schedule by the "Rhythm Method" 171

21. ARE YOU GETTING ENOUGH SLEEP?
Learn How to Get the Sleep You Need 173
Are You Getting Enough Sleep? 173
The Five Stages of Sleep. 175
   . . . and the Things That Go Wrong in the Night . . . 176
So, What Should *You* Do about Sleeping? 177
Six Steps for Getting a Good Night's Sleep. 178
   1. Avoid Nicotine, Caffeine, and Alcohol 178
   2. Take Sleeping Pills Short-Term or Not at All . . 178
   3. Keep Regular Meal Times. 179
   4. Stick to Regular Bed and Rising Time. 179
   5. Exercise Regularly 179

6. Don't Worry about It 180
If Sleeplessness Persists 180
Is It a Problem or Just a Pattern?.............. 180

22. LOSING THE WAR ON STRESS?
Learn How to Declare a Truce 183
The Parable of the Mice in the Refrigerator....... 185
The Fun Stuff Is Also Stressful 185
The Bozo Factor 186
Stress Happens 188
Being Blessedly Stressed 188
Three Great Lies of Our Age.................. 189
The Fundamental Truth about Stress 190
    You Have to Incur Stress to Lose Stress....... 190
    One Size Does Not Fit All 190
How *You* Can Reduce Your Stress Levels 191
    1. Acknowledge and Honor Your Feelings 191
    2. Find Safe Ways to Express Your Feelings ... 191
    3. Unplug 192
    4. Fix It............................ 192
    5. Create Quiet Time Alone—Every Day 193
    6. Plan Your Escape Routes................ 193
    7. Wallow in Successes and Pleasures........ 193
    8. Give Less Than 100 Percent 194
    9. Create a Third Basket 194
    10. Do One Thing at a Time 194

23. WHAT, YOU WORRY?
Learn How to Stop Letting Worry
    Rob You of Time and Energy................. 197
Three Ways to Worry 197
Measuring the Worth of Worry 198
10 Ways to Get Rid of Your Worries 199
    1. Don't Resist or Deny the Fear............. 199
    2. Name It as You Claim It 199

3. Consider the Consequences. 199
4. Push the Worry to the Max 200
5. Figure Out What, If Any, Action You
   Will Take 200
6. Follow Through 201
7. Abide by Your Decision 201
8. Realize You Are Not Alone in Your Anxiety. . . 202
9. Act in Spite of Your Fear. 202
10. Protect Yourself from the Worry Contagion. . 203
The Five Faces of Worry. 203
1. Worry Festering Out of Ignorance. 203
2. Worrying Lurking in the Future. 203
3. Worrying Focused on the Past. 204
4. Worry Feeding on Inertia 204
5. Worry Thriving on Evasion. 204
What to Do When It's More Than Worry 204

24. WHEN'S THE LAST TIME YOU HAD AN IDEA?
Learn How to Make Time to Think 207
Why You Shut Yourself Off from Your Good Ideas. . . 208
Welcoming the Ah-Ha! 208
Creating the Ah-Ha on Demand 209
Step 1. Make a Creativity Appointment 210
Step 2. Tell Your Subconscious What You Want. . . 210
Step 3. Stay Alert. 211
Step 4. Play with the Possibilities. 211
Step 5. Stop Before You Have To 213
New Age? Nonsense. 214

25. WHAT ARE YOU REALLY LIVING FOR?
Create a Values-Based Time Management Plan. . . . 215
Does the Way You Spend Your Time
   Truly Reflect Your Values?. 216
   The Myth of "Quality Time" 216
Are You Mistaken about Your Priorities?. 217

Why Aren't You Spending Time on the
Important Stuff?. 218
1. Time Spent Making Money Is Time
Spent on the Family 218
2. Working at Your Job Is Easier
Than "Working at" Your Family 219
3. Social Pressure Rewards Traditional
Concepts of Work 219
How to Live a Values-Centered Life 219
Step 1. Create a Personal Mission Statement . . . 220
Step 2. Define Values in Terms of Actions 220
Step 3. Schedule for Your Values 221
Step 4. Go Gently into That New Life 221

Index 223

Preface

I wrote this book in my "spare time."

Yeah. Right.

I wasn't able to put the rest of my life on freeze-frame while I wrote it. In fact, work has been like a swarm of bees. (We're "reorganizing" in the face of serious budget cuts.) Writing the book was "extra."

I wrote it because I needed it.

I've read everything on time management I could get my mitts on. A lot of the techniques helped me a lot—and I've included a great deal of traditional time management lore here.

- You'll learn how to create a to-do list that really helps you get things done without driving you nuts.
- You'll learn why you might be having trouble saying "no" to extra tasks now and how to say "no" effectively.
- You'll learn how to separate, organize, and, yes, eliminate, tasks.
- You'll learn how to tame the technology, so that it saves rather than waste your time.

Much of what we call "time management" seems wrong to me, wrong and even dangerous, especially when it urges us to accept nonsense like, "You can do more with less."

You can't do more with less, friends. If you do more of one thing (like work), you'll do less of something else (like sleep).

If you try to do too much for too long, you're going to make yourself sick.

I developed my own way of "managing time" (which is to say "living") because traditional time management was making some bad things in my life worse—the sense of constant pressure, the breathless rushing from one appointment to the next, the desperate checking of items off the endless to-do list.

That's why this time management book contains material you won't find elsewhere, lifesaving tips like:

- How to put the power in the pause—taking several "mini-vacations" each day to break the stress cycle
- How to turn a wait into a rest
- How to get your ideas down on paper or up on the screen—quick
- How to create a desktop where you can see the wood
- How to put off putting it off
- How to deal with the bozos who frustrate you and steal your time
- How to deal with stressors so you can decrease stress
- How to get enough sleep and rest

So, welcome to a kinder, gentler time management, one designed not to help you do more and more and more but to enable you to do the right things better—and still have time and energy left for the fun stuff that never gets put on the to-do list.

Everything in this book is based on one simple premise: you get to decide what to do next.

Take a deep breath. Get ready to look at your life honestly. I'll suggest. You'll decide.

Deciding is what time management is really all about.

MARSHALL J. COOK
marshall.cook@ccmail.adp.wisc.edu
Madison, WI
April 1997

Acknowledgments

Ellen Malloy Cook shares her life with me, puts up with my rather unorthodox approach to time, fills my home with laughter and furry creatures, provides a warm, safe haven from a world that often seems anything but warm and safe. She is my joy and my consolation. As always, this book is for her.

This particular book owes its existence to John Woods, an editor who gets things done, and a man with a passion for ideas and a vision for the workplace. And all books on time management (by any name) build on the wisdom of Alan Lakein and thrive on the good work of folks like John Robinson and Juliet Schor.

Chapter 1

Do You Have Speed Sickness?

Learn to Detect Adrenaline Addiction and
Other Symptoms of the Madness

Are you old enough to remember the plate spinner on the old Ed Sullivan variety show? This haggard-looking fellow would charge onto the stage, balance a plate on a pole and set it spinning, repeating the deed with a second pole and plate and then a third. About that time, the first plate would slow down and start to wobble, so the spinner would hurry back to the first pole and rev up the plate, give numbers two and three a little goosing, and then start a fourth plate spinning.

The idea was to get fifteen plates spinning at once without letting any fall. This accomplished, the fellow would run down the line, snatching all the plates off the poles, to the thunderous applause of the audience.

I remember as a kid thinking how hard it must be to learn how to be a plate spinner. I also remember wondering why anybody would want to do something so pointless and nerve-racking.

We've become a nation of plate spinners. But unlike the pro on the Sullivan show, we seem to break a lot of plates, and we don't get any applause on those rare occasions when we manage to keep all of the plates spinning.

How about you? Is the tape of your life stuck on fast forward? Is your game plan a perpetual two-minute drill complete with no-huddle offense? Have you developed FedEx dependency because you're behind in your work?

1

You could be suffering from speed sickness—and not even know it.

Speed sickness isn't really new. Cracker-barrel philosopher Will Rogers defined it as well as anybody when he observed, "Half our life is spent trying to find something to do with the time we have rushed through life trying to save."

Here's a simple test to see if you're suffering from speed sickness. All you need is a partner to keep track of time while you estimate how long it takes for one minute to elapse. Sit down and get comfortable. No fair peeking at a watch, and no fair counting off "One Mississippi, Two Mississippi . . . ." Your partner says "Go." When you think a minute has passed, you say "Time's up!"

Go ahead and try it. Then read on to find out how others did.

How far did you get? Did you underestimate the amount of time you had waited? If so, you're in the majority. In monitored tests, most folks called out "Time's up!" after only about 15 seconds. At least one subject thought the minute was up after just seven seconds. Very few made it a whole minute.

If we were as bad at estimating space as we seem to be at estimating time, we'd be crashing into each other all the time.

Here's another test. Just sit still and do nothing for one minute, 60 little seconds, while your partner times you. How long does that minute of enforced inactivity seem to you? Are you uncomfortable with just one minute of stillness?

A minute has become an eternity. We measure time in nanoseconds now. (A nanosecond is one billionth of a second.) A supercomputer performs hundreds if not thousands of operations in one trillionth of a second. One trillionth!

One more test. It takes a little longer than the one-minute drill, but it isn't difficult, and it doesn't require a partner. Simply leave your watch at home when you go about your business tomorrow. At the end of the day, reflect on these two questions.

1. Did you find yourself checking your wrist even when you didn't want or need to know what time it was?

2. Even without your watch, did you have any trouble keeping track of time?

If you answered "yes" to the first question and "no" to the second, you're again in the majority. Most of us have become accustomed to tracking time in ever smaller increments as we drive ourselves from task to task, deadline to deadline, appointment to appointment. We even schedule the fun stuff. This constant checking has become habitual, so we don't even realize how time-driven we've become.

I left my watch on the dresser one morning about four years ago and, with rare exceptions, have left it there ever since. I found myself glancing almost compulsively at my naked wrist for several days, a wave of anxiety washing over me each time I realized I didn't have my watch on. And yet I found that I always knew what time it was.

In our culture the trick is to *avoid* knowing what time it is. Reminders are everywhere. Clocks leer down at us from office walls, and watches bob on the wrists of almost everyone we meet. The fellow on the radio chirps out the time constantly, in artless variations. ("It's seven sixteen, 16 minutes after the hour of seven o'clock, 44 minutes before eight ....") Our computers blink the time at us when we log and keep track of every passing minute while we work. Neon signs blink the time and temperature at us as we drive to our next appointment.

Pause for just a moment to consider this: at one time there were no clocks and no watches. When the first public clock was erected in a village in England, folks flocked to the town square to view the wonder. And it only had one hand! You could tell time only to the nearest hour.

Can we even imagine life without the timekeepers? Probably not. We're not just aware of time, we're driven by time, besotted with time, engulfed in time.

"Time is on my side," Mick Jagger and the Rolling Stones told us in the 1960s, but time has become both the elusive prey and the hunter, chasing us through the day, the week, the year. "Slow down, you move too fast," a more mellow group, The Lovin' Spoonful, advised, but we didn't listen.

RIDING THE ADRENALINE HIGH

Here's another simple test to diagnose a possible case of speed sickness. Just respond "yes" or "no" to the following statement: "I work better under pressure."

A lot of us seem to think so. We claim the trait on our resumes (along with "highly motivated self-starter"), and we brag about our ability to perform under the tightest of deadlines.

I've written on deadline all of my adult life, and I've prided myself on my speed and accuracy under pressure. In my younger days, I even flirted with those deadlines, seeing how close I could cut it, getting that one last interview before sitting down at the keyboard and blasting off.

It wasn't just the constant caffeine creating that heady buzz. I was on an adrenaline rush akin to an amphetamine high. And in that giddy state, I honestly believed I was doing my best work while I rode the crest of my momentum.

You, too? Go back and look at that work after you've calmed down. Your best? If you're honest with yourself, you'll admit that the quality of the work suffers when you race through it.

And *you* suffer, too. You've got motion sickness—not the kind that causes queasiness when you react to the rolling of a ship, but rather a physical and psychological dependence on motion and speed that can become almost as powerful as a true addiction.

"Leisure time" has become an oxymoron. We experience one long workday, broken but not relieved by gulped meals and troubled sleep. Only the models in the clothing catalogs seem to have time to lounge.

We Americans take shorter and fewer vacations, and we take our work with us, with our beepers and cell phones, faxes and e-mail. Home computers only began to sell, remember, when

IBM had a Chaplinesque "Little Tramp" show us how to "take work home on your fingertips."

"Leisure" no longer rhymes with "pleasure" as we race through life, checking the "fun" items off the to-do list. Even our play has become purposeful (physical conditioning or enforced "relaxation") and competitive (who plays golf without keeping score?). I even read recently about a birdwatching competition.

Birdwatching? Competition?

SIMPLE SYMPTOMS AND SCARY CONSEQUENCES OF SPEED SICKNESS

How about you? Have you got a case of motion sickness? Symptoms include:

- nervousness
- depression
- fatigue
- appetite swings
- compulsive behavior (repetitive actions that are difficult or even impossible to stop)
- unwillingness and even inability to stop working
- inability to relax even when you do stop working

That's not good, but it's not lethal. Hold on. It gets worse. We all have to run the occasional sprint, meet the unyielding deadline, cope with the unforeseen emergency. And we can do so effectively and without long-term damage. It can even be exhilarating.

But keep driving in that fast lane until it becomes a way of life and you run the risk of

- hypertension
- heart disease
- drug dependency
- stroke

Rushing through life suppresses the immune system, hampering the natural formation of T-lymphocytes (white blood cells). That, in turn, opens you up to a variety of ills, some categorized as "psychosomatic" ("all in your head"), but all very real.

Life in the fast lane can make you sick. It can even kill you.

REPORTS OF THE "DEATH OF WORK" PREMATURE

In an article in a 1959 issue of *The Saturday Evening Post*, highly regarded historian and social commentator Arthur Schlesinger, Jr., warned Americans of "the onrush of a new age of leisure." Warned? In 1967 noted sociologists came before a U.S. Senate subcommittee on labor to predict with great confidence that Americans would soon be enjoying a 22-hour work week or a 22-week work year. Many of us would be retiring at 38, these experts said, and the big challenge, as Schlesinger indicated eight years earlier, would be in handling all that free time.

These prognostications remind me of the executive at Decca Records who turned down the chance to sign a garage rock band from England because "guitar music is on the way out."

The band was The Beatles, and they have done okay with three guitars and a set of drums. The only one on the way out was the Decca exec.

How could the "experts" have been so wrong? What happened? Why didn't our marvelous technology usher in the Age of Leisure?

We took the money. We opted for a higher material standard of living instead of time off.

You don't remember making that choice? Perhaps it was never offered to you, at least not in those terms. But by and large most of us decided to work more rather than less, and more of us went to work, so that instead of the Age of Leisure we created the Age of Anxiety and the norm of the two-income household.

Women, in particular, got caught in the time crunch. You were supposed to be able to have it all, a thriving family and a successful career. But too many superwomen came home from a hard day at the office only to find all the housework waiting for them. They wound up working, in essence, a double shift, all day, every day. And single mothers never had a choice. If they didn't do it, it didn't get done.

Whether or not we made the choice consciously, there was plenty of pressure on us to choose the money. Hard workers get and keep jobs as well as social approval. When the boss advises us to "work smarter, not harder," she really means "get more done," and that means working harder as well as smarter. "You can do more with less," we're told when asked to take over the workload for a departed colleague (no doubt a victim of "downsizing," or even "rightsizing"). But it's a lie. You can't do more with less. You can only do more work with more time, effort, and energy, and that time, effort, and energy have to come from other parts of your life—like conversation, sleep, and play.

WE HAVE SEEN THE ENEMY, AND IT IS US

Is it all the bosses' fault? Not really. In many ways we've inflicted speed sickness on ourselves.

We use our busy-ness as a measure of our self-worth and importance. We define our sense of purpose and our meaning in terms of our to-do list. We've internalized the clear social message that busy people are worthy people, even morally superior people. ("Idle hands are the devil's workshop.")

It isn't just peer pressure. Deep down inside us, stillness makes us nervous. Many of us actually dread free time and secretly look forward to Monday morning (although we'd never admit it). Unstructured time is threatening, and so we fill up the hours—all of them.

We abhor the notion of "wasting" time and speak of "saving" time, and "spending quality time," as if, as the adage has it, time were money, or at least a commodity like money, capable of being either stashed or squandered.

So where is that "time" you've "saved"? You can't see it. You can't hold it in your hands. You can't put it in a box and hide it for safekeeping.

JUST WHAT *IS* TIME, ANYWAY?

"If no one asks me, I know," St. Augustine once replied to this question. "If they ask and I try to explain, I do not know."

Here's a simple way to find out what time is to you. Jot down several phrases that use the word "time" in them. Make them descriptive of the way you relate to time. For example, you might write

> "I'm trying to learn to spend my time wisely," or
> "I've found that I can save time by making a to-do list every morning before work," or
> "I tend to waste time after dinner."

Go ahead and take a moment to write a few. (This is a *work* book, all about you working out *your* relationship with time. I promise the exercise has a point.)

Now rewrite each statement, but substitute the word "life" for the word "time" and see what you come up with.

In our examples above, we'd get

> "I'm trying to learn to spend my life wisely."
> "I've found that I can save life by making a to-do list."
> "I tend to waste life after dinner."

The point to this little parlor trick? (Did you think of it as a "waste of time"?) If even one of your revised statements startled you, even a little bit, you got the point. We aren't talking about some tangible commodity when we discuss the time of our lives. We no more "have" time than we "have" inches of height.

We're talking about our very lives.

Time is nothing more (or less) than a way of measuring out that life. Other cultures measure time other ways, and some cultures don't measure it at all.

Here are how some other cultures speak of time:

"Think of many things. Do one." Portuguese saying
"Sleep faster. We need the pillows." Yiddish saying
"Haste has no blessing." Swahili saying
"There is no hand to catch time." Bengali saying
"Today can't catch tomorrow." Jamaican saying

And here's our own beloved bard, William Shakespeare, advising us from a long-gone time: "O, call back yesterday, bid time return!"

Can't be done. So, how "much" time do you really "have"? In one sense, we each have exactly the same "amount." We have the moment we're living right now. That's all. And it's everything.

That's not to say we shouldn't learn from the past and plan for the future, even if we can't store it or hold it. We're going to do a great deal of learning and planning as we explore time together. However, although we remember the past and envision the future (both highly creative acts), we can't live in either one of them.

You can only live now as well as you can (by whatever definition of "well" you develop). This book is designed to help you do that, and you have more choice in the matter than you think. To a great extent, you get to decide how you live right now.

You can use this basic checklist, four questions to help you make those decisions:

1. What has to be done?
2. How much of it has to be done?
3. How fast does it have to be done?
4. How much does it cost to do it?

The answers to these questions will enable you to decide what to do now. These decisions will add up to your whole life, well lived.

Chapter 2

Are You Really as Busy as You Think?

Find Out How You're Really Spending Your Time

Are you working longer and harder now than you used to?

You said "yes," right? Most do—especially those who buy books on time management.

Juliet Schor agrees with you.

In her 1991 best seller *The Overworked American*, Schor notes that the shrinking American work week bottomed out at 39 hours in 1970 before it started to rise. She says we now work an extra 164 hours—one full month—each year. She also notes the rise in the two-income household in the last 25 years. While we're putting in those longer hours on the job, there's no one at home to clean and cook and plan a social life.

The average American works two months a year more than do most Europeans, she adds. Four weeks of vacation a year are mandated by law in Switzerland and Greece, for example, and workers in France and Spain must have *five* weeks. Actual vacation time is often a lot longer (five to eight weeks a year in Sweden).

Schor blames the increase in working hours on the eclipse of unionism and a slowdown in economic growth, making it necessary for folks to work longer just to maintain their standard of living.

That seductive lifestyle has, in fact, trapped us in what Schor calls the "insidious cycle of work and spend." We work longer to make more money to buy more stuff. She concludes that we must "reclaim leisure."

In 1985 John Robinson thought we already had.

As head of the Americans' Use of Time Project at the University of Maryland Survey Research Center, Robinson had been keeping track of how we spent our time since 1965.

In that time, Robinson says, we actually experienced a steady *increase* in free time. Men gained an average of seven hours of leisure each week, up to 41 hours, and women were right behind them with a six-hour gain to 40 hours each week to call their own.

We think we're busier, he notes, but it just isn't so. "The perception of a time crunch appears to have gone up in the period of time where free time has increased," he concludes.

Surprised? So was Robinson, since his findings run counter to what we say about our lives.

A NATION OF WATCHERS AND SHOPPERS?

How can we have more leisure time but feel more rushed? Watching television eats up 37 percent of the average American woman's spare time and 39 percent of a man's, Robinson reports. Perhaps time spent passively absorbing those flickering images somehow doesn't register as "leisure," and we subconsciously subtract it from free time, the time we feel we can choose to spend as we wish.

Robinson expected to be able to categorize folks according to the way they spend their free time. One man would be likely to work on his car engine, he reasoned, while another would rather go to the ballet.

But that's not what Robinson found. It isn't a matter of either/or. It's much more a case of all or nothing. The split Robinson uncovered is between the doers and the sitters. The same folks most likely to attend cultural events, for example, are also more likely to fix their own carburetors. Others don't seem able to report having put their free time to any particular use.

Robinson explains this split between the doers, or "omnivores," as he calls them, and the do-nothings in terms of one of

Newton's laws of physics: Bodies in motion tend to stay in motion; bodies at rest tend to stay at rest.

Robinson himself is an omnivore. Along with a rigorous work schedule, he makes time to go to jazz festivals, search for old miniature golf courses, and test locally brewed beers.

So who's right? Are we Schor's worker bees or Robinson's couch potatoes?

Recent findings reported in *American Demographics* magazine for June 1996 back both conclusions. The percentage reporting having "less free time than five years ago," after keeping time-use diaries in 1995, was a whopping 45, backing Schor's contention. But that figure was down from 54 percent in 1990, bearing out Robinson's assertion.

The same article cites the increasing popularity of cats over the more dependent and time-intensive dogs as evidence of our busy-ness, by the way.

Even Robinson agrees that, whatever the reality, we *feel* busier. His Use of Time Project survey in 1985 reported 32 percent of us "always feel rushed." By 1992, the figure had risen to 38 percent in a survey by the National Recreation and Parks Association. Think about that. Almost two out of every five of us report *always* feeling rushed.

The numbers soar for certain categories. It is not surprising that working mothers topped the charts in the 1992 survey with a 64 percent "too busy" self-rating. No matter what Robinson says, I suspect working mothers feel they're too busy because they *are* too busy.

However much free time we have, a two-year Gallup Poll bears out Robinson's contention that we spend a lot of it in front of the tube. Watching TV ranks way ahead of any other leisure-time activity, from 26.2 percent on Sunday to 34.1 percent on Thursday. Reading and socializing vie for second place, with 8.9 percent (or 5.29 hours a week) for socializing on Fridays.

If you can't find us in front of the television, Schor suggests you try the shopping mall. We spend three to four times as many hours a year shopping as do Western Europeans, she reports, and the United States now contains 16 square feet of shopping center for every man, woman, and child in the country.

All that shopping takes money, of course, and we've got it. The average American's yearly income of $22,000 is about 65 times the incomes of about half the world's population, Schor notes.

We work to earn to spend. When not earning or spending, we relax in front of the tube. And we say we don't have enough time.

HOW ARE YOU "SPENDING" YOUR LIFE?

This book is about you. So how about it? Are *you* too busy? Are you wasting too much time? That's not up to Robinson or Schor or Cook or anybody else to decide. You get to decide what's a waste of your time. And you get to decide how you're going to spend that time.

First you need to know how you're spending your time now—not the "average American" from Robinson's surveys, and not some hypothetical wage-slave in Schor's studies—*you*.

Are you willing to take a close, honest look at the way you spend your time (which is to say, the way you live)? If you don't like what you find, will you use the results to redirect your efforts and energies?

To do so takes effort and self-awareness. It also takes courage.

Get yourself a notebook just for this exercise. Make sure it's portable, fitting in purse, coat pocket, backpack, or attaché case. You'll want to have it with you all the time. On the first page of that notebook, list the major categories you want to track. Your list will be different from mine or anybody else's.

Certainly we'll all include the same basic categories, such as "sleep." (I've never met anyone who doesn't sleep, at least some of the time, although a lot of us don't sleep as much as we'd like to or think we should. More on that in a later chapter.)

But you may want to differentiate between "bed sleep" and "nap-in-the-living-room-recliner sleep," for example.

We'll all have "eat" on our lists of basic time-consuming activities, but again, you may want to split food time into regular sit-down meals, eat-and-run drive-through raids on nutrition, and foraging (or snacking or noshing or whatever you call it).

Is "work" specific enough for you? It depends on how much you want to learn from this self-study. I suspect most of us will want to keep closer tabs on exactly what we're doing at work, breaking time into categories such as "meetings" (perhaps also differentiating between "productive meetings" and "total-waste-of-time meetings"?), "report writing," "responding to telephone inquiries," "commute time" (*Don't* forget commute time, which may be a major and previously unnoted time-consumer), and even "break time." (Don't be afraid to chart breaks. You may well discover that you take too few rather than too many.)

The more categories you create, the more precise and helpful the information and the more annoying keeping track will be. The more you decide to put in, the more you'll get out later. Err on the side of overscrupulous data-keeping. The information you collect here is going to serve you well.

Let your list sit overnight and take another look at it, adding and deleting as you see fit. Have you forgotten anything? You can, of course, add items during your survey week if you haven't anticipated everything here. The key is to note the items you're interested in tracking and to be sure your system enables you to account for your time fairly accurately. (It will do no good to list two hours a day as "miscellaneous.")

Give each item on your list a number, a letter, or both. "Work" (as in job) could be 1, for example, and "going to waste-of-time meetings" could be 1-A. But keep it simple. The system should help you gather data, not get in your way.

You're almost ready to start your self-study. First, write down your estimate of how much time per week you spend in each category. You can do this in total hours, in percentage of time spent, or both. When you're done, you'll probably want to convert hours into percentages anyway.

For example, if you figure you average seven hours of sleep a night, you can write "49" (7 x 7) next to that category on your list. Since there are 168 hours in a week, 49/168's computes to 29 percent (actually, 29.167 percent, if you need to be that precise. On the other hand, "about 30 percent" may suit your purpose).

Next to your estimate, write the number of hours/percentage you think you *ought* to be sleeping each week. If in your heart of hearts you believe that Mom was right, for example, and that you really do need eight hours of sleep, you'd write in "64/33.3 percent" next to your "49/29 percent."

Now keep your time log for a full week. Try to pick a "typical" week (if there is such a thing), neither vacation nor business trip, and relatively free of major crises. If a crisis does erupt in the midst of the week you've chosen, you can always start over another week.

It is important that you be persistent and precise.

Can you do two activities at once? Of course. In fact, traditional time management books insist you do two, three, even four things at a time. But for the purpose of this survey you're going to decide on the dominant activity at any given time. For example, if you're listening to a book-on-tape while driving to work your dominant activity is "driving to work." The book-listening is incidental. If you're reading a book with the television on, you need to decide whether you're mostly reading a book or watching television.

Start your log when you wake up on Day One.

6:15 A.M. Lay in bed, semi-conscious, "listening" to "Morning Edition."

Make your next notation when you significantly change your activity.

6:32 A.M. Dragged carcass out of bed. Bathroom. Shower. Dress.
6:58 A.M. Breakfast.

The smaller the increments, the more precise the results (and the more work the gathering).

> *6:59 A.M. Worked crossword puzzle*
> *7:02 A.M. Stopped working crossword puzzle to let dog out in backyard.*
> *7:02:15 A.M. Resumed working crossword puzzle.*

Too precise? I doubt you'd find this level of precision desirable or helpful. I also doubt you'd keep recording that way for a full week. Make your notes in a way that will tell you what you want and need to know about yourself at the end of the week.

Be honest, even if it hurts. Folks tend to fudge downward on time spent watching television and upward on time spent exercising, for example. You want a true picture of your activities in a typical week. Then you can decide if you want to change anything.

Try not to let the process of keeping track of time alter the way you actually spend that time. This can be hard to do. If you know you're going to have to record it, you may be less likely to want to flop down and watch a "Wheel of Fortune" rerun from "Hollywood Starlets Week." But if that's what you would have done without the log, that's what you ought to do with it.

Nobody has to see your log, and you have the power to change anything you don't like about the way you live (and to decide to embrace anything you do—public opinion be damned).

Allow enough time at the end of your survey week to do the math. (No, you don't have to note this time on your log. You're finished with that.) Go back to your first page, where you made your list and created your Estimate column and your "should" (Ideal) column, and write in the Actual numbers. Each entry should now have three sets of numbers after it.

	Estimate	**Ideal**	**Actual**
Sleep	49/29%	64/33.3%	52/31%

If you've been rigorous and honest, you may get some surprises:

	Estimate	Ideal	Actual
Internet/e-mail	7/4.2%	7/4.2%	68/40.5%

Okay. You're not likely to get that big a surprise. But you may note some relatively large discrepancies among estimates, ideals, and actuals. If so, rejoice. You're a perfect candidate for time management. You may find that by adjusting actual times to conform more closely to your ideal, you'll improve your life significantly.

You may also find that you need to rethink some of your ideal times and your reasons for having established them.

If an adjustment leaps out at you now, note it in a fourth column, "New Ideal," or "Time Management Goal":

	Estimate	Ideal	Actual	New Ideal
Internet/e-mail	7/4.2%	7/4.2%	68/40.5%	14/8.4%

Then write the adjustment you intend to make in the form of a declaration:

> *"I will surf the Internet and answer e-mail no more than two hours a day,"* or
> *"I will average no more than 14 hours on-line each week."*

Congratulations. You've taken the first big step in successful time management. You've accounted for your time. You've perhaps uncovered areas where you may be spending too much of that time and areas where you aren't spending enough. You've made some initial declarations concerning your future activities. If you did nothing else, this new level of self-awareness and resolve would be extremely helpful to you.

But there's much more you can do, if you're willing, to help yourself spend time wisely and well; not to satisfy the numbers on the chart, but to create a joy-filled as well as productive life.

Chapter 3

Can You Really Manage Time?

Learn What to Control and What to Let Go

We define time management as a personal rather than a social issue in our culture. Stressed out? Too busy? That's your problem. Take care of it. Or don't. Just be sure to pay your bills and show up for work on time.

But let's think on a social level for a moment before we buckle down to the job of changing one single life: yours.

As a culture, could we establish a six-hour work day, a 30-hour work week, and a paid vacation for every worker (maybe not Sweden's five to eight weeks, but something)?

Could we support alternative working arrangements such as flex time and job sharing?

Could we acknowledge workaholism as a true social disorder instead of a badge of honor?

If not, are we willing to count the true price we pay as a society for health care—mental as well as physical—along with underemployment and unemployment?

Impossible, you say? In the 1950s we decided that fighting the threat of a Communist takeover was our most important priority, and we completely restructured society to do it. (An important reason President Eisenhower created the interstate highway system, for example, as a means of evacuating our cities in the event of a nuclear attack.)

In the early 1960s John F. Kennedy pledged that the U.S. would have a man on the moon within the decade, and we did it.

Check out the way social attitudes have changed toward cigarette smoking in the last 20 years. That didn't just happen. Folks worked hard to change those attitudes.

Huge changes in social awareness and values are possible. What about changes in the way we evaluate our usefulness and care for ourselves?

But for now, you need to work on the one part of society you really can change—you.

JUST WHAT *CAN* YOU DO ABOUT THE TIME CRUNCH?

"YOU CAN'T CONTROL YOUR BOSS,
YOUR WORKLOAD,
YOUR WEIGHT,
YOUR BACKHAND,
YOUR WEEDS,
YOUR DOG,
YOUR LIFE," a recent Microsoft ad proclaims in thick block letters. The punchline:
"AT LEAST NOW
YOU CAN CONTROL
YOUR CURSOR"

Advertisers don't promote feelings or advocate lifestyles. They sell things by connecting with existing feelings and adapting their products and services to dominant lifestyles. The folks at Microsoft aren't saying we *should* feel out of control. They're assuming that we do—and offering a partial solution, an island of tranquillity in an ocean of chaos, one good product that works the way it should.

Let's examine the premise. Can you "control" your boss? (Would you want to if you could?) Is your workload totally beyond your control? You *really* can't do anything about your weight (diet and exercise?), your backhand (practice, practice, practice—or give up the damned game), your weeds (pull 'em—

or hire somebody to do it for you—or take out the lawn and put in a nice rock garden), your dog (don't let my friend Patricia McConnell, a professional pet behaviorist, hear you say that)?

Picture the frenzied worker in another recent ad, obviously pushed to within an inch of her breaking point. *"When you work late at the computer, do your contact lenses crash?"* the headline probes. The solution: *"They won't crash if you use Opti-Free."*

I recently appeared on *The Oprah Winfrey Show* to talk about time and stress management. One of the other guests was a professional waiter. No, not the fellow who describes the special quiche of the day and keeps your water glass brimming. This patient fellow is working his way through college by standing in line as a surrogate for people willing to pay him to do it while they're off doing other, presumably more important, tasks.

"If there was a SPEED LIMIT on how fast a person could work you'd be breaking it," a breathless ad for frozen food gushes, "but there isn't so you just keep going faster...and good thing you have a QUICK MEAL."

These examples represent one dominant approach to time management. When you're too busy, buy your way out with a product or service to help get you through physically, mentally, psychologically.

But here again, we should tally the true price for such conveniences, in time and money spent shopping, in increasing dependence, in the missed pleasures of cooking and smelling and savoring (and, in many cases, *chewing*) food. We have to count up the toll—on our eyes and stomachs and psyches—when we push ourselves to work ever harder, ever faster, ever longer.

When you start keeping score right, sometimes you'll also start changing some of the decisions you make.

LIMITS TO THE TRADITIONAL TIME MANAGEMENT APPROACH

"You can gain extra minutes and even hours every day by following these tips from a time management expert," the article in the tabloid newspaper announces. (You know the kind of paper I'm talking about, the kind nobody reads, let alone buys, but that somehow boasts a paid circulation in the millions.)

Among these tips from the expert, Lucy Hedrick, author of *365 Ways to Save Time*:

- "If you don't have time for reading, letter-writing, cooking or exercising, get up earlier in the morning."

That seems to be a favorite solution. Other experts, the ones who study sleep, estimate that Americans are now getting 60 to 90 minutes less sleep each night than they did 10 to 15 years ago. (Again, more on the vital topic of snoozing in a later chapter.)

- "Keep your breakfast fast and simple. Try a 'blender breakfast' consisting of a banana, fruit juice, granola and a dash of honey."
- "If your bathtub needs a cleaning, do it during your shower. You can scrub as you finish washing or while your hair conditioner is working."

I *could* do those things. I could make up a huge pitcher of "blender breakfast" and keep it in a cooler in my car, so I could drink it on the way to work.

I could take a water-proof tape player into the shower with me, so I could listen to a self-help tape (preferably on one of those compressed players that takes the "dead air" pauses out) while I'm going at the grouting with my toothbrush. I suppose I could even wear my clothes into the shower, like the protagonist in Anne Tyler's marvelous novel, *The Accidental Tourist,* so I could wash my duds while I showered, grouted, and listened.

But I'm not going to do any of those things. I'm not saying they're bad things. They might work wonderfully for some folks. But I personally would pay too high a price for the saved seconds.

I have to chew my breakfast, so I know I've really eaten; I'll have to live with the inconvenience and the irrevocable passage of time while I chomp my Grape Nuts.

I want and need the three-minute oasis of a steaming hot shower, my little morning miracle, a pleasure for body and soul, to start even the busiest day.

I do, however, get up at 5:00 and exercise for 45 minutes to an hour and a half every morning before I chew my way through breakfast and wallow in that hot shower. That works for me. It might not work for you.

Lots of folks take a Walkman with them when they jog. I prefer letting my mind drift. Comedienne Joan Rivers reportedly has a speakerphone on her treadmill. More power to you, Joan. Whatever works. But that sounds awful to me.

Some of you need to impose strict order on your work space—a place for everything and everything in its place, with neat files, a clean desktop, a floor you can actually walk on. I'm in the compost heap school of desktop management, and I don't mind hurdling the piles of files and books and periodicals that inevitably collect on the floor.

I even found support for my slovenly workplace. In *How to Put More Time in Your Life*, Dru Scott extols "the secret pleasures" of clutter, calling messy folks "divergent thinkers" (which, you have to admit, sounds much better than "messy slob").

The classic rules of time management don't work for everyone. You have to find your own way through the suggestions and exercises that follow. You may not be able to control some elements of your life—and you may not want to.

There are lots of things none of us can control. If you drive a car anywhere more populous than the outback of Australia, you're going to get stuck in traffic. Manage the flow of traffic? You might as well try to manage the current of the river in which you swim.

If you make an appointment, somebody's going to keep you waiting. A phone solicitor will interrupt your dinner. Your boss will dump a last-minute assignment on you. Your child will get sick the same day you have to make that mega-presentation before the board.

SO THAT'S WHERE THE TIME *REALLY* GOES!

Efficiency expert Michael Fortino offers the following dismal scenario for the average life lived in these United States. In your lifetime you will spend

seven years in the bathroom,
six years eating,
five years waiting in line,
three years in meetings,
two years playing telephone tag,
eight months opening junk mail, and
six months sitting at red lights.

You'll get interrupted 73 times a day(!), take an hour of work home, read less than five minutes, talk to your spouse for four minutes, exercise less than three minutes, and play with your kid for two minutes.

Nightmarish. Want to change that picture? Just as with poor Scrooge, scared into life change by the ghosts of Christmas past, present, and to come, it's not too late for you to refocus your life. That's what time management is really all about.

But no matter what you do, you're still going to spend a lot of time waiting at red lights, idling in waiting rooms, and standing in line.

SOME INITIAL CHANGES TO GET CONTROL OF YOUR TIME

You could make huge changes. You could quit your job, leave your family, move to a cabin in the Dakotas and paint landscapes. You *could*. But you probably won't and probably shouldn't.

You can make tiny changes, without needing anybody's help or permission. You can, for example, learn to take four mini-breaks a day, as I'll suggest in a later chapter.

You can explore the possibilities for some mid-size changes, involving the cooperation of other people in your life. Could you, for example:

- take your next raise in time rather than money or advancement?
- work at least part of the time at home?
- substitute barter and skills-swapping for cash for some of what you need?

As you work your way through this book, let yourself explore as many possibilities as you can. Some won't be practical. Some won't work for you. Some will be beyond your means, for a variety of reasons. But by applying your creativity, initiative, and energy to this exploration, you will find ways to create meaningful, life-affirming change.

Chapter 4

Do You Run the List, or Does the List Run You?

Learn to Use the To-Do List Effectively

There's nothing new about the to-do list. Folks have been jotting down lists of things they need to do and then checking each item off the list as they do them for a very long time. The more you need to do, and the more pressure you feel to do it, the more helpful the list can be.

Alan Lakein spelled out the uses and misuses of the to-do list in his groundbreaking 1973 book, *Time Management: How to Get Control of Your Time and Your Life*. He showed us how to prioritize those to-do items, making sure we tackled the essential items first. Lakein's idea was to use the list to get everything done, starting with the important. But the overall goal was to live a happy, healthy, well-rounded life. Lakein had the wisdom to consider rest, recreation, and relationships as important components of the full life.

Subsequent time management coaches seem to have lost Lakein's gentle wisdom and sense of proportion. The to-do list has become a means of fitting ever more work into the same limited 24-hour day. The list has become a tyrant, pushing us to DO MORE instead of helping us to do better and to do right.

Time management consultant Anne McGee-Cooper identifies the resulting sense of frenzy in her book *Time Management for Unmanageable People: The Guilt-Free Way to Organize, Energize and Maximize Your Life*. When you try to get more done in the same amount of time, she counsels, you run the risk of overload, a phenomenon known in computer lingo as "thrashing," when the computer gets too many commands at once and gets stuck trying to decide what to do first.

There are other dangers inherent in developing a list of tasks the night before or during the morning of each workday. To illustrate those dangers, let's look at a sample to-do list, one that makes just about every possible mistake. Here, then, is

THE TO-DO LIST FROM HELL

We'll impose a mid-level of organization, less than a minute-by-minute script but more than a simple list of tasks.

To do before work
> Exercise: 100 sit-ups, 50 push-ups, 25 squats
>
> Review agenda and materials for staff meeting
>
> Read *The Wall Street Journal*

Morning commute (17 minutes)
> Listen to motivational self-help tape on time management

Morning
> Answer faxes, overnight mail, voice mail, e-mail (8–9)
>
> Staff meeting (9–10:30)
>
> Organize research for quarterly report (10:30–11:45)
>
> Drive to lunch meeting (15 minutes)
>
> Lunch meeting (noon–1:30)

Afternoon
> Write draft of quarterly report
>
> Meet with committee on workplace expectations (3–4:30)
>
> Afternoon commute (18 minutes—pick up dry-cleaning)

That's it. There's your workday, all laid out.

Do all that and you'll likely be laid out, too.

Notice that your ability to accomplish all the tasks on your list depends on split-second timing. Everything must go perfectly—no traffic jams, no emergencies, no interruptions.

When's the last time you had a perfect day—no traffic jams, no emergencies, and no interruptions?

That's what I thought.

THE DAY AS YOU REALLY LIVE IT

You sleep through the snooze alarm twice. (You're exhausted from your wrestling match with yesterday's to-do list.) No time for exercise or, for that matter, breakfast—which didn't even make it onto the list. You're down two, feeling guilty and grouchy before you've even gotten started.

You glance at your meeting notes, skim the left-hand column on the front page of the *Journal*, and sprint to the car. You're in luck. The car starts, even though you've put off getting it serviced—no time. No idiot ruins your day by getting into an accident ahead of you, and traffic flows fairly smoothly.

Even so, the commute takes 18.5 minutes, so you're already running 90 seconds behind. You didn't get to listen to your motivational tape, either, because the tape deck in the car jammed. (Better put "get tape deck fixed" on your future to-do list.)

You can anticipate the rest. (You don't have to anticipate it. You've *lived* it.) You don't get anywhere near through the voice mail, let alone the e-mail. The meeting starts late and runs long—don't they always? It's too late to tackle the quarterly report, and you spend the rest of the morning answering the phone and battling faxes, most of which could have just as well come by snail mail—or pony express, for that matter. (What makes us think our stuff needs to be communicated instantly?)

After a lunch you didn't taste and a meeting you didn't need, you finally get a few minutes for those notes for the quarterly report. You're tired, grouchy, full of a chicken enchilada that refuses to settle down and let itself be digested, and preoccupied with the meeting you've got to get to in a few minutes. No wonder the report refuses to organize itself.

Another meeting (starts late, runs long), another snarling, gut-wrenching commute, a wasted stop at the dry-cleaners (in your rush this morning, you left your claim ticket on the bureau).

Another day shot.

And now it's time to start the second shift, the workday put in at home sweet home.

Pretty dismal scene, isn't it?—and not really that much of an exaggeration.

Did the to-do list help? Sure. It provided a record of what you didn't get done while you were doing other things, and it helped you to go to bed guilty and frustrated by every unchecked item.

What went wrong? You failed to plan for the unplanned. You weren't realistic about your own capacities or about the real time required to do things. You left stuff off the list that nevertheless needed to be done.

In short, this wasn't a to-do list. It was a wish list, a fantasy, an unattainable dream, an invitation to frustration and fatigue.

I hadn't read Lakein's book or McGee-Cooper's when I started using the to-do list as a way of getting some control of the chaos, and I made just about every idiot mistake you could make. If I can keep you from making the same mistakes, it will make my day.

10 SUGGESTIONS FOR CREATING A HEALTHY TO-DO LIST

1. Don't Put Too Much on It
This is fundamental. Master this one, and everything else falls into place.

Be realistic in your expectations and your time estimates. Make a real-world list, not an itinerary for fantasyland. Otherwise, you'll spend the day running late, running scared, just flat-out running to catch up. You won't even have time to notice how your efficiency drops as you become cranky and exhausted.

Don't jam the list. Let it help you organize, keep on task, and get the job done.

If by some miracle things take less time than you had allowed for, rejoice! You've given yourself the gift of found time, yours to spend however you want and need to.

To help follow rule #1, follow rule #2.

2. Put Some Air in It

Overestimate the commute time. Figure in the wait before the meeting, the time spent on hold, the traffic backup.

3. List Possibilities, Not Imperatives

This speaks more to your frame of mind when you make the list than to the specific notations on that list. You're listing those tasks that you hope, want, and, yes, need to finish during the day. You're not creating a blueprint for the rest of the universe, and your plans don't have the force of natural law.

What happens if you don't get to everything on your list? What happens, for example, if you wake up simply too ill to crawl out of bed, let alone tackle the crammed workday?

I'm talking serious sick here, not the borderline sore throat and headache that might keep you in bed on a Saturday but not on a workday. In a way, the serious sickness is easier, because you don't have to decide whether or not to attempt to go to work, and you don't have to feel guilty about staying in bed while the rest of the world is tending to business. (Depending on your tolerance for pain and your level of guilt, you might have to be near death to achieve this state.)

Let's suppose you're sick enough to have to stay flat on your back in bed for two days, and you can barely wobble around the house in bathrobe and slippers on the third. In all, you miss an entire week of work.

Meanwhile, what happened to the stuff on your to-do list?

The meetings went on without you. Folks figured out they could live without the quarterly report for another week. (It was that or write it themselves.) You've got 138 unheard messages on the voice mail (62 of them from the same person), 178 items in the e-mail box (52 of them the result of a list server getting "stuck" and sending out the same message multiple times), and a desk awash in memos, faxes, overnight letters, and other unnatural disasters. You take stuff home for a week, trying to get caught up.

That's bad. It isn't *that* bad. You didn't die. You didn't lose a loved one. Western Civilization did not grind to a halt. Commerce and government managed to struggle on without you.

It's too late to respond to some of those urgent memos and messages, but it turns out they really didn't need response after all.

Try to remember that the next time you're relatively healthy but nevertheless falling behind on the day's tasks.

Think you've had a bad day at the office? Consider former Los Angeles Dodger center fielder Willie Davis, who met his own personal disaster during the second game of the 1965 World Series against the Baltimore Orioles. In the top of the fifth inning of a 0–0 tie, with Dodger ace Sandy Koufax on the mound, Davis managed to make three errors in one inning, including two on the same play, to blow the game. The Dodgers never recovered, losing the series in four straight games.

After his record-setting game, Davis was philosophical. "It ain't my life," he told a vast radio and television audience. "And it ain't my wife. So why worry?"

Another baseball player/philosopher, Satchel Paige, put it this way: "Don't look back. Something might be gaining on you."

We say things like:

"Don't sweat the small stuff...and it's all small stuff," and
"In a hundred years, who'll know?"

But we don't really believe or act on such adages.

None of this is to suggest that what you do isn't important—at least as important as playing baseball. I'm simply saying that you, and I, and everybody else, need to keep things in proper perspective.

4. Don't Carve the List on Stone Tablets

When I first started making a to-do list each day, I'd type the list into my computer and run it off on the laser printer. What a beautiful and impressive document it was, with crisp black letters on clean white stock, a regular work of art.

That was the problem. I wouldn't draw a mustache on the Mona Lisa, and I wouldn't cross out or rearrange anything on a laser-printed to-do list.

Your list has to be flexible if it's going to do you any good. You have to be able to change it, digress from it, flip it on its ear, add to it, wad it up and toss it in the recycle bin—if it's really going to help.

Find a flexible format that works for you. If you like an intricate grid system, with squares for every five minutes during the day, go for the grid. If crayon on butcher paper is more your style, start scrawling.

Don't try to fit a format. Find or create a format that fits you.

5. Order Creatively

Make sure the most important tasks get done before you drown in a sea of relative trivia. Answer the e-mail first if it's the top priority on your list. If it isn't, schedule it for later in the day. Don't do it first simply because it's there, demanding attention, or because it's relatively easy, or because you've gotten into the habit of doing it first.

Vary your pace, alternating difficult and easy, long and short, jobs requiring creative thought with rote functions. Change activities often enough to keep fresh.

Attack mentally taxing jobs when you're most alert and energetic. (We'll talk about biorhythms in a later chapter.)

6. Break the Boulders into Pebbles

When I first started editing my newsletter, *Creativity Connection*, I boxed off an entire afternoon on my calendar to "DO NEWSLETTER." I had carefully counted backwards from the publication date to allow for printing and mailing, and I figured a full four hours was plenty of time to write and edit the material and lay it out in PageMaker.

I was, of course, being an idiot.

Folks didn't get their copy in on time.

I didn't get mine written on time either.

When I finally got the first page laid out, it disappeared into the ether. (Where does all that stuff go after it disappears from the computer screen?)

The longer and later I struggled, the deeper into the mire I sank. When I finally got done, I was a mess. So was the newsletter.

I no longer schedule a session to "DO NEWSLETTER." I schedule several sessions, one to write, edit, and lay out the reviews, another to select and edit reader letters, another for the writer profile, and so forth. I prepare the market updates relatively close to final deadline to keep them current, let the finished pages sit and cool off for at least a day, make my final read through and send it to the printer.

I've even gotten so I rarely launch a page layout into the cosmos.

The newsletter comes out in much better shape. So does its editor.

7. Schedule Breaks, Goofs, Time-Out Time, and Little Rewards

Most of us schedule "rest" for last—if we schedule it at all. By the time we get to it—if we get to it—it's too late to do us any good.

If you don't put rest on the list, you won't do it. So put it on the list. And don't save it for last. Plan the rest for when it will do you some good, before you become too tense or exhausted. Brief rests at the right times will help you maintain a steady, efficient work pace.

Instead of waiting until the end of the day for that 15 minutes of pleasure reading, for example, schedule three five-minute reading breaks during the day. You may even want and need to schedule that game of catch with your kid or that walk around the neighborhood with your spouse.

I know—that sounds awful. What kind of monster has to schedule things like that? Lots of us monsters. Instead of calling yourself names, start planning a balanced, fulfilling life.

8. Schedule for Long-Range as Well as Short-Term Goals

You know you should do some serious financial planning. You know you should have a current will. You know you should create a systematic plan for home maintenance and repair.

If you know all that and never seem to get to it—put it on the schedule.

9. Be Ready to Abandon the List

"If you only write the story that is planned," writer and teacher Ellen Hunnicutt tells her students, "you miss the story that is revealed."

The same goes for the story of your life. The most important thing you do all day, all year, or even all lifetime, may never appear on any to-do list or show up on the dayplanner. Never get so well organized and so scheduled that you stop being alert to life's possibilities—the chance encounter, the sudden inspiration.

Not all surprises are bad surprises. It just seems that way sometimes.

For a delightful depiction of the dangers of developing list addiction (which surely must have its own 12-step programs and support groups by now), read "A List," one of Arthur Loebel's delightful Frog and Toad stories. (I know. Frog and Toad are for kids. So are Horton, that wonderfully faithful elephant, and Ferdinand, the goofy bull who would rather smell the posies than gore the matador. And they remain among my favorite tales.)

"I have many things to do," Toad realizes one morning. "I will write them all down on a list so that I can remember them."

He writes down "wake up" and, realizing that he's already done that, crosses it off—a great momentum-builder.

Other items include "getting dressed," "eating breakfast," and "going for a walk with Frog."

Disaster strikes, as it must in any great work of literature. While Frog and Toad are on that walk, a gust of wind snatches the paper from Toad's hand. Like Dumbo, who thinks he can't fly without his "magic" feather, poor Toad finds himself incapable of acting without the list to guide him.

Toad's story has a happy ending, but I won't spoil it for you. You'll just have to make the time to read it for yourself.

10. You Don't Have to Make a List at All

The to-do list is a tool. Techniques for creating an effective list are suggestions, not commandments. If they help, follow them— adapting and modifying to fit your own circumstances and inclinations. If they don't help, make your own kind of list, or don't make any list at all. You won't have "failed time management." You'll have simply discovered something that helps some folks and not others and which doesn't turn out to be helpful to you.

Bonus Suggestion: Create a Not-To-Do List

Along with noting and organizing the tasks you'll do, you might also want to write down those things you *won't* do.

I'm not talking about the sorts of epic life-pledges that appear on lists of New Year's Resolutions, stuff like: Stop smoking, Don't nag, and Cut consumption of chocolate. You can certainly make that kind of list if you find it helpful, but I'm referring here to day-to-day tasks that have fallen to you by custom, habit, or lot but that should properly be done by someone else or not done at all.

Examine large tasks (serving on the school board) and small ones (responding to every memo from the district supervisor) to make sure (1) they need to be done and (2) you're the one who needs to do them. If the task fails on either count, put it on the *not*-to-do list.

Time management isn't just or even primarily about doing more things in the same amount of time or doing the same number of things in less time. Time management also involves choosing to do the *right* things.

Chapter 5

Getting Started:

Learn How to Jump-Start Each Work Session

Most of us suffer to some extent from work-aversion. Some of us like our work, and most of us at least don't hate it, but we'd still rather be doing something else most of the time.

That's why they call it "work," right?

That aversion makes getting started the hardest part of any job.

"Writer's block" gets the most press, but folks encounter "executive's block" and "plumber's block" and "computer pro-grammer's block," too—that state of semi-paralysis brought on by fear and pain and just plain old lack-of-want-to.

We all have to learn to work through the aversion if we want to maintain the habit of eating regularly. But some of us perform time-consuming start-up rituals before we start to work, and many don't really work effectively for several minutes even after starting.

You may not even be aware of your rituals, which makes them hard to get rid of. Some of your warm-ups may actually help pre-pare you to work, but others may simply postpone the inevitable confrontation. Those are a waste of time, and you need to get rid of them. Here's how.

SEVEN WAYS TO GET A FAST START

1. Prepare Mentally

Back at the turn of the century, a man named Charles Haanel called the subconscious mind "a benevolent stranger, working on your behalf." For all our subsequent research on the working of the brain, I've yet to encounter a better description.

You can get that subconscious stranger working for you on any job you have to perform.

The night before the job, tell your subconscious exactly what you want to accomplish the following day. You're not issuing orders here. You're not telling the subconscious how you intend to do the job. That's part of the conscious planning stage.

You're simply planting the idea, giving that larger mind that exists outside of conscious thought time to mull and sift, combining images and ideas, amassing energy and positive attitude.

Instead of letting the subconscious disaster tapes play, visualize yourself performing exactly as you wish. This is particularly helpful if you're going to speak to a group or otherwise put yourself before an audience.

This isn't a matter of "wishing will make it so." Positive visualization won't cast a magic spell over your audiences. But it will affect *your* behavior, helping you call forth your best effort by concentrating energies and consciousness.

For some great athletes, this ability seems to be a natural gift, no less than speed, strength, and coordination. They talk about a strange kind of prescience during which they seem to see themselves hitting the home run, intercepting the pass, or returning the backhand baseline volley before they actually make the play.

What comes to some as gift you can claim as tool.

2. Prepare Physically

You should have your physical tools assembled and accessible before you begin the job. If possible, stake out a specific place for the work, where you can keep everything you need within easy reach and leave stuff out between work sessions. That way, you eliminate time spent pitching camp and then tearing it down again each time.

Also, when you become accustomed to doing a job in a specific place, you'll be focused and ready to work as soon as you enter that place. It doesn't have to be fancy or even private. It just has to be yours, and it has to have the tools you need.

3. Map the Terrain
Before you begin the trip, figure out where you want to go.

Remind yourself of your purpose. What's in it for you? For your organization? For the client or customer? If you can't answer these questions, save yourself time and effort—and ensure that you'll do a better job—by taking a few moments now to get the information you need and to focus on what you hope to accomplish.

If you still aren't sure, seek out the authorization, approval, or verification you need. Again, a few minutes spent here can save hours later. And you'll work more efficiently and confidently.

If the work involves several stages, write them down first. Don't try to create the sort of orderly outline only an English teacher could love. Just jot down the steps or ideas in the order they occur to you. Then number the items in proper sequence.

4. Start Anywhere
If you aren't ready to start at the beginning, start someplace else.

You can't escape certain sequences. A plumber has to turn off the water before disassembling the pipes, for example. But jobs often contain a great deal of flexibility. The finished product has to be assembled in the proper order, but you don't necessarily have to tackle the components in that order.

A director shoots a movie in the most practical sequence, getting all the location shots before returning to the studio for the interiors, for example. These separate scenes become the raw material for the finished movie. If the director and the editors do their jobs well, the viewer can't tell (and doesn't care) in what order the scenes were shot; the movie tells a coherent, entertaining story. The seams don't show.

When you're thinking your way through a problem, it doesn't matter where you start. It only matters *that* you start.

5. Start Anyway

I've known lots of writers who have suffered from blocks at one time or another. Poets seem especially susceptible to the disease.

But the working stiffs who write on deadline day after day never seem to get blocked.

Lots of times they write when they feel lousy. Lots of times they worry that lack of time has forced them to do a lousy job. Folks who can't afford to get writer's block don't get it.

The same goes for plumber's block, CEO's block, and bus driver's block.

The poet can afford to wait for inspiration. The rest of us do the job, inspired or not.

If you're good at your work, a professional in the best sense of the word (whether or not you're getting paid), your mood doesn't show in the finished product. Nobody can tell whether or not you felt like doing it. Fact is, they don't even care. They're interested in the results, and the results can be just as good regardless of the mental anguish you felt dragging yourself to the task.

6. Lock Out the Critics

We all make mistakes. We writers get to make ours in private, and we can give ourselves the chance to fix them before anybody else sees them. But when Green Bay Packer quarterback Brett Favre throws an interception, half the known universe sees him do it (or so it seems in football-crazy Wisconsin), and there's no way he can pull the ball back and take the play over.

But I know of lots of writers who compose their rough drafts as if a Lambeau Field full of rabid fans and multiple millions of TV viewers were watching. Even worse, they write with their editors perched on their shoulders, ready to pounce at the first sign of a dangling modifier.

Maybe you're doing your job that way, too, feeling the eyes of editor or boss or critic while you try to think your way through a challenge.

It's a two-step process, first the doing, and then the judgment. Just as an NFL quarterback has to shut out the howling of the mob and concentrate on the receiver, you have to shut out concerns about judgment during the process of creation. If you don't, you won't take a chance, try out an idea, risk a "failure" in the eyes of the invisible judge.

You might even be afraid to start—and getting started is the only way you'll ever finish.

7. Stop Before You Need To

"Don't stop me. I'm on a roll."

Momentum is a wonderful feeling, especially when we've got a lot to do and not much time to do it. The last thing you want when the job is going well is an interruption. Common sense tells you to keep working until you're finished. If you can't finish the job in one sitting, you work until you're exhausted or until you run into a snag you can't work your way through.

But it actually makes a lot more sense to stop before you get too tired and before you reach a snag.

We'll explore the benefits of resting before you need to in the next chapter. For now, we'll talk about the savings in start-up time. If you stop because you're stuck, you carry that "stuckness" with you until the next work session. And if you give yourself too much time, you'll build up an aversion to the task, the very material blocks are made of.

But if you've stopped in mid-stride, sure of the next step you'll take, you'll come back to the job confident and even eager. You won't have to waste any time getting back into the groove, because you won't have gotten out of it.

We'll learn how to get maximum benefit out of minimum break time in the next chapter.

Chapter 6

Is Your Life a Constant Two-Minute Drill?

Learn How to Call Time Out— and Put Power in the Pause

It's the most exciting—and the longest—two minutes in football. The trailing team has the ball and hope but no time-outs. The quarterback (we might as well put John Elway in there; he's the best ever at pulling the game out in the last minute) drives his team down the field, working the clock and the sidelines, eating up yardage while preserving time. There's no time to huddle or even to take a breath. It's just take the snap, drop back, and throw.

For a football fan, the two-minute drill is a joy to watch. But as a way of living, it has its drawbacks.

YOU KNOW YOU'RE RUNNING YOUR TWO-MINUTE OFFENSE WHEN . . .

- You charge from meeting to meeting, appointment to appointment, with no time to gather your thoughts;
- You've taken lunch at your desk so often, your keyboard gets clogged with bread crumbs;
- The ringing phone makes you jump;
- You feel one bad surprise away from throwing up your hands and screaming;

- A long-time friend calls to tell you she's coming to town and would love to see you, but you make excuses because there's just no way you can spare the time;
- You aren't getting any exercise, but you feel exhausted;
- You crawl into bed at last—and can't fall asleep.

We all go through days, even weeks like that. For short spells, it can even be exhilarating—as long as we can keep one jump ahead of disaster. But the longer you sustain this killer pace, the more you suffer and the less efficient you become—not just in your work but in every aspect of life.

If you wait for life to ease up and for the bad surprises to stop coming, you may wait too long. You have to call an end to the two-minute drill, for yourself, your loved ones, and your colleagues. But the more you worry about relaxing, the more tense you become. What now?

WARNING: MAJOR METAPHOR SHIFT HERE FROM THE FOOTBALL FIELD TO THE SURF

I grew up in southern California, and so of course I surfed. It was required. (I didn't own a Woody, and I never bleached my hair, but I *did* listen to a lot of Beach Boys music.) I had a couple of scares, and one in particular when I went body-surfing when the lifeguard was flying the yellow flag for caution.

The waves didn't look so bad from shore. But one of them took my measure, sucking me toward it with a savage undertow. I managed to catch the wave, but the curl at the crest drove me straight down and under. I hit bottom and spun completely around. I hadn't gotten much of a breath before I was pulled under, and my lungs were already fighting for air. I realized with what was left of my wits that I literally didn't know which way was up.

I started thrashing desperately, fighting the current and exhausting what was left of air and energy.

All my thrashing was actually holding me in place against the current and my body's natural tendency to rise in salt water. Had I kept struggling, I might not be here to tell you the story. Some instinct or impulse (or possibly just simple fatigue) stilled me. I went limp—and immediately began to rise toward the surface.

I had saved myself by doing nothing.

And that's what I suggest you do to save yourself. Relax mind and body and let the current carry you for a couple of minutes, four or five times a day. This inspired nothing will save you.

PUTTING THE POWER IN THE PAUSE—TAKING MINI-VACATIONS EVERY DAY

Take your break before you need it. Don't wait to be exhausted, and don't wait to be stuck. Break your momentum—and the buildup of stress and fatigue—with a sanity break in the midst of the chaos. Make the break a good habit, three or four times a day.

Here are six simple break activities (and an advanced technique for you fast learners) that work for me. After you read them, jot down three or four more of your own.

SEVEN WAYS TO GO ON VACATION WITHOUT LEAVING YOUR DESK

1. The Breath Break

Here's about the simplest, cheapest vacation you'll ever take. For two minutes, just breathe. Take air way down into your belly. You should actually be able to feel your stomach rise with the intake of breath.

But haven't you been breathing already? Sort of. But as you hurry, and as you feel the pressure build inside you, your breath becomes shallow, and you don't get the oxygen you need. You'll especially notice this when you have to speak in front of a group. Your voice rises and gets squeaky, and your throat becomes dry and sore.

To combat the ill effects of this oxygen debt, you don't have to empty your mind or chant a mantra or wrap yourself into a yoga position. All you have to do is breathe deeply and slowly for a couple of minutes three, four, even five times a day. In private, with your feet up and your eyes closed would be nice, of course, but you can take a breath break in the middle of a meeting, behind the wheel of the car, or on the phone. Nobody needs to know you're sneaking oxygen.

2. The Continental Drift

Think of a place of perfect contentment in your life, "your own special island," as Bloody Mary sings in "South Pacific." Harken back to a time when you were truly relaxed and at peace. Or create an imaginary oasis.

Then go there for two minutes.

Shut everything else out, close your eyes, and create the scene in your mind. See, hear, feel. Let warmth and peace wash over you.

You'll return refreshed after just a couple of minutes, and you'll know you can go back again soon.

3. Pack Up Your Troubles

Something bothering you? Get rid of it.

Picture your nemesis, hot branding iron in hand, sneering at you, ready to poke and prod. If your anger and frustration has an abstract source, give it specific shape. Lack of time making you crazy? Picture a clock gone berserk, its hands spinning out of control. Or make time into a huge Indiana Jones–style boulder, rolling toward you with desperate speed.

Then put the image into a bubble and imagine that bubble floating slowly up and away, becoming smaller and smaller until it finally disappears.

Action-movie alternative: Forget the gentle bubble stuff. Blow your troubles to smithereens.

Hey? Are you starting to enjoy this? Good. That's what vacations are for.

4. The Shoulder Shrug

We tend to take out our tensions on specific parts of our bodies. Shoulders are one of my favorite targets. Without knowing I'm doing it, I tense my shoulders as I work. If I don't catch myself at it, I end up with a sore neck and shoulders and a pounding headache.

I can break the tension, save my shoulders, and avert the headache by remembering to relax my shoulders and rotate them slowly and gently for a couple of minutes. On particularly bad days, the results are dramatic. My shoulders seem to drop several inches, and a soothing warmth flows up my neck.

I never even realize how tense I am until I unclench my muscles and relax. How about you? Are you tensing and clenching while you work?

5. The Phrase for the Day

This one takes a bit of preparation, but it's well worth the effort. Collect pithy bits of wisdom, interesting observations, intriguing fragments of ideas, funny phrases, anything that snags your fancy. You can catch them everywhere—from the media, from conversation, from your own boundlessly creative and endlessly curious mind. Get in the habit of jotting them down as you run across them.

When it's time for a break, pull one of your gems out, read it a couple of times, and let yourself chew on it for two minutes. Don't direct your thoughts. Just let them wander where they will.

6. The Object of Your Affection

Hold a picture of a person you treasure, an object that has special meaning for you, or a talisman (like that lucky silver dollar you've lugged around with you for years). Spend two minutes with it, again letting your thoughts roam.

These six work for me. What might work for you? Why not take a two-minute break and jot some ideas down?

7. Advance Resting Technique, for the Gifted and Talented
Combine the breathing with any other relaxation activity.

WHY THE TWO-MINUTE BREAK WORKS
Will a two-minute break really do you any good?

Yeah. It really will. But you may feel uncomfortable breathing from your tummy the first few times, and you may not notice the effects right away. But if you stick with it, you'll feel the difference.

Here's why.

As you come under fire in the daily wars, your body instinctively reacts, tensing muscles and doling out emergency rations of adrenaline and other natural uppers, getting you ready to fight your enemies or run away from them. These automatic responses will work against you when you've got no one to fight and nowhere to run.

These reactions can build on themselves, and you can get caught in a dangerous loop. You sense danger, and your body responds. That response in turn seems to verify the perception of danger and triggers still more response.

No wonder you can't relax at the end of the day!

But the cycle can work for as well as against you. If you can relax your body—slowing your breathing, calming your heart—by taking a two-minute break, your panic will subside. You'll regain focus, clarity, and energy.

FREE 21-DAY SATISFACTION-GUARANTEED TENSION TRIAL
I can assure you that these techniques have helped me greatly. You can prove that they work for you by trying them for 21 days before drawing any conclusions about their effectiveness. Break up your day with three or four of these short breaks for three weeks and see if you notice the difference.

But I'll warn you right now: you won't remember to rest on your own. You're going to have to build these breaks into your daily routine, and you'll probably even need to plant reminders, in the form of a note in the briefcase, a Post-it on the refrigerator, an alarm clock. (Setting an alarm to remind you to rest?! Whatever works.)

If you hang around a computer most of the day, as I do, you might be able to program your inanimate partner to remind you, with a beep or a scroll line ("Don't forget to relax!") or some such.

How about it? Are you willing to try? You have nothing to lose but tension and that "quiet desperation" Thoreau warned us about so many years ago.

Chapter 7

If You Don't Know Where You're Going, How Will You Know When You Get There?

Learn How to Get Organized

For some of us, trying to get organized is neither easy nor natural. But it's necessary for anyone who wants to use time effectively.

Are you a TP or a CL?

To keep things simple—always a good idea for effective time management—we'll separate everyone into two categories of organizers, the TPs and the CLs.

Your classic TP tends to be Tidy and Punctual. TPs keep a neat work and home space. They don't drop it on the floor; they put it in its place. If a CL drops it, the TP will probably pick it up.

A place for everything, and everything in its place—that's the TP motto. Socks get neatly folded and put in the drawer designated specifically for socks and nothing else.

TPs tend to be detail-oriented and perfectionists. They'll see a project through step by step, checking and rechecking as they go. They have a tough time going on to the next step until the one they're working on is completed to their satisfaction.

TPs are punctual. If they say they'll be there at 1:00, they arrive at or before 1:00. Because they place such a high value on being on time, some TPs tend to become impatient with folks who don't, one reason why interaction between TPs and CLs is not always pleasant.

If you like a TP, you'll describe her as "conscientious," "well-organized," and "meticulous."

If you don't like the TP, you'll use words like "picky," "uptight," and "rigid" (or worse).

Everything the TP is, the CL, well, isn't. CLs tend to be Cluttered and Late.

The CL figures if God had wanted clothes hung up, She wouldn't have invented gravity. Besides, the CL knows exactly where everything is, or so she says.

Where the TP likes a well-regulated buffet, the CL seeks out the stew.

CLs ignite with excitement in the idea stage of a project but tend to flame out when it comes time to implement.

When the CL makes an appointment for 1:00, it's a rough estimate.

But the portrait of the CL shouldn't be all negative. Some CL traits tend to correlate highly with characteristics also associated with creativity and divergent thinking:

- Tolerance for chaos and ambiguity
- Ability to accept failure
- High energy and enthusiasm
- Willingness to laugh, especially at him- or herself

If you like the CL, you probably think of him or her as "laid back," "easy going," and "flexible." But if you're the one who has to pick up after the CL, your descriptors might be "slob" and "inconsiderate jerk" (if not worse).

In Neil Simon's "The Odd Couple," sportswriter Oscar Madison is the classic CL trying to coexist with super-TP Felix Unger.

ASSESSING YOUR PERSONAL STYLE

By now you've probably found yourself in one category or the other—perhaps squirming a bit as you did.

Fact is, you're neither all TP or all CL. Each of us is a mixture of traits, and any categorization of human beings will always be an oversimplification.

Human characteristics aren't either/or; they present a range.

Very TP   Balanced   Very CL

If you want a little help in figuring out where you place on the TP/CL continuum, give yourself the bathroom test.

Hold on. This probably isn't what you think.

Take a look at the bathroom after you get done with it in the morning. Have you squeezed the toothpaste tube carefully from the bottom and did you remember to recap it when you finished? Did you rinse off the toothbrush and hang it up in its place? For that matter, have you replaced that toothbrush within the last three months (the way dentists suggest we should)?

Or did you swish a little water around in your mouth and spit (assuring yourself that you'd brush extra well next time)?

The first description is very TP and the second very CL.

You wouldn't think of using the last of the toilet paper and not replacing it with a fresh roll—would you? A CL might ("I am in a hurry here!"), but a TP, no way.

How many rolls of toilet paper do you have in reserve? A TP will have plenty of tp, is in fact much more likely to run out of room to store the extra rolls.

Is your bathroom routine unvarying from day to day (always done at the same time, in the same order)? Or is every morning a catch-as-catch-can adventure?

And yes, men, the eternal question of the toilet seat probably enters into our calculations here. If you live with somebody who cares whether you put the seat back down when you're finished, even if it doesn't seem like that big a deal to you—your compliance may say something about you on the TP/CL scale.

If you don't bother to lift the seat up before you let fly, you're definitely on the CL side of the line. So, who's right?

From our description, it might seem pretty clear that the conscientious TP is a much better citizen than the flighty CL. We all remember the fable of the grasshopper and the ant, right? The good ant prepares for winter, while the bad grasshopper will have to rely on the kindness of strangers when the snow starts to fall.

But this isn't about right and wrong, moral or immoral. One way isn't right (thus implying that the other must be wrong). One group isn't better than the other. They're just different. We see and evaluate life differently, and we react out of our perceptions.

To thrive, most organizations need a mixture of types, folks with the TP's virtues of conscientious, sustained effort and precision, and folks with the CL's creative flair for innovation.

And like the successful organization, the efficient, effective individual blends TP and CL traits, with organizational skills that don't dampen zeal and playfulness.

HOW TO SEE THE FOREST *AND* THE TREES

Your basic "very TP" personality is superb at handling the details, tying up the loose ends, keeping the train on track and running on time.

The "very CL" sees the big picture, focusing on where those tracks lead and whether we really want to go there.

In shaping your life, scheduling your activities, and planning how you will spend your time, you need to take care of both the details and the overall direction those details lead you in.

Never lose sight of your basic goals, those ultimates that underline your life and give it its meaning. What's really important to you? Family? Spiritual growth? Financial security? Health? Phrase these values, your personal mission statement, as precisely as you can. No one has to ever see, much less judge, these statements. This is just for you. Use your CL skills here to see the scope of your life. It's quite a mural.

To the extent that you're able to organize your life around these fundamentals, you'll be able to achieve satisfaction.

But if you're to achieve your goals, you need to break those goals into specific steps, those steps into activities, those activities into a schedule that invites and facilitates action.

And that brings your TP self into play.

BREAKING GOALS INTO STEPS

Let's suppose one of your basic life goals is to "maintain good health and physical fitness." Who could argue with that? By now most of us know that physical well-being bears directly on mental health, mood, and ability to work and play.

Now—what, specifically, are you going to do about it?

After a bit of concentrated brainstorming, let's suppose you come up with these steps:

1. Lose 25 pounds.
2. Exercise regularly.
3. Drink alcohol in moderation.

Good start. But now you have to define these steps much more clearly.

"Lose 25 pounds" seems straightforward enough, but even this goal requires a little refinement. Why do you need to lose weight? Why 25 pounds? How fast is safe? How will you maintain the loss when you achieve it?

And, of course, losing weight is going to come down to the day-to-day matter of what and how much you put into your mouth. Are you going to try a prescribed diet or a weight loss program with prepackaged foods? Or are you simply going to "cut down" or "give up dessert"? You need to get specific.

"Exercise regularly" is also vague.

Define "exercise." Does it have to hurt to be good for you? Does parking the car at the far end of the lot and taking the stairs instead of the elevator constitute sufficient exercise?

What does "regularly" mean? Every day? Twenty minutes with your heart rate at 80 percent of its maximum three times a week? (Such precision appeals much more to the TP personality, as does the record keeping that may go with it.) A little jogging when you have a chance? (More in line with CL thinking.)

Whatever your personality, you need to break your laudable goal of regular exercise into specific activities, based on a realistic appraisal of your capabilities, the options available to you, and your tolerance for various forms of exercise. (You can say you're going to swim laps for an hour a day, but you'll never do it if you aren't at least an adequate swimmer, if you don't have easy access to a pool, or if lap swimming bores the daylights out of you.)

Considering such factors, suppose you develop this exercise regimen:

1. Work out on the treadmill for 30 minutes three times a week.
2. Ride the exercise bike for 30 minutes three times a week (alternating with treadmill).
3. Do light-weight, aerobic weight lifting for 30 minutes twice a week.

As a part of your plan, you also need to decide what you won't be doing while you're lifting weights or riding that exercise bike. You aren't adding a half an hour to the day, after all. You're taking that time from someplace else.

Will you get up a half an hour earlier, skip lunch, shun your daily session with Dan Rather, Peter Jennings, or Tom Brokaw?

Now you've got a specific plan. All that remains is the doing.

"All," he says!

SCHEDULING THOSE STEPS

Get out the calendar or the day planner.

Work around your work schedule, of course, but don't automatically assume that you can't move some of your work obligations to accommodate your exercise.

Also factor in family and other personal obligations and rhythms. Missing dinner at home for that workout at the Y will help you achieve your fitness goal but rob you of family time.

Finally, as much as you can, accommodate your biorhythms. I exercise first thing in the morning, which seems to suit me fine and gives me energy for the rest of the day. But my regimen might be all wrong for you, and might cause you to abandon your high resolve before you've given yourself a fair chance.

When you've settled on appropriate times for exercise, write them down on the calendar, and train yourself to consider these "appointments" to be as important as any others you make.

That means that the sort of emergency that would cause you to miss a doctor's appointment or a board meeting would also keep you from your exercise session. So would significant illness or injury. But if "I don't feel like it" or "something else came up" wouldn't keep you from your performance review with the boss, it must not keep you from your self-made appointments, either.

When you begin your new routine, give yourself plenty of reminders. In addition to the notations on the calendar and the day planner, you might want to plant Post-it note "land mines" where you're sure to stumble over them during your normal work routine. Some folks can even program their computers to give them periodic reminders. Give yourself visual clues—like a sweat band next to your wallet or purse in the morning.

Be firm in your resolve. Soon the exercise—or any other addition to your schedule—will become a happy habit.

EVALUATION

How will you know if it's working?

Give yourself enough time. It takes at least three weeks to get over the novelty and the discomfort of breaking patterns and beginning to establish a new routine.

Record your reactions in a notebook. You'd be surprised how much your reaction will change in just a few weeks, so much so that you might forget how you felt when you started.

Keep referring to your specific goals. Are you losing that pound and a half a week? Is your new exercise regimen giving you the increased energy and sense of well-being you hoped for?

Evaluate, too, how the change is fitting into the rest of your life. How are your loved ones reacting to the new demand on your time? What have you had to give up to create time for the new activity? Is it a fair trade-off?

Decide to stick with the plan for another three weeks, make necessary alterations, or scrap the plan and develop a new one. These are your goals, and you have the power to achieve them through specific planning and disciplined action every day.

Chapter 8

Is It Really Important—
or Merely Urgent?

Learn How to Create Order from the Daily Chaos

What next?

You face that question hundreds of times each day, from the moment you wake up until you lapse back into sleep. Your answers to those questions determine how you live your life. The sum total of all those answers *are* your life.

Many of the questions are pretty basic yes/no decisions:

Shall I get up now or stay under the covers for just a few more minutes?

The answer to a simple question can branch into a more complex set of choices. If you decide to eat breakfast, your next question is, of course, "What shall I eat?" A Spartan bowl of oatmeal, no brown sugar, no butter, no syrup? A chocolate glazed donut? Two eggs fried in bacon grease? Cold meatloaf between two leftover pancakes?

Shall I take a shower? If I take a shower, shall I wash my hair? If I wash my hair, shall I use conditioner?

Shall I wear clothes today? If I wear clothes today, what clothes shall I wear?

These aren't really choices, you say? Of course you get up each morning, at pretty much the same time, at least on weekdays. Of course you eat breakfast, or not, as is your custom. And of *course* you wear clothes. You don't have any choice about something like that.

Ah, but you do. I insist that you have a choice.

Take the matter of clothes. Almost everybody in our culture wears them, at least in public. This is a matter of law and custom. Where I live (Wisconsin), it's also a matter of survival during several months of the year.

You do have a choice, however. The consequences of going naked among your fellows far outstrip (sorry, couldn't resist) any potential benefits, yes, but you could still make the choice, just as you could choose not to go to work (and sometimes do, when illness or life events tip the balance in that direction).

More obvious is the choice of what clothes to wear. Your clothes make a statement about your position in society and your attitude toward your fellows. If I wear a suit, tie, and wingtips, I announce that I'm a solid and productive citizen on my way to business. If I wear a ragged sweatshirt and cutoffs, I still might be a solid citizen, but I'm planning on doing some gardening or washing the car. Black leather, lipstick, and spiked heels make an entirely different statement, especially when worn by a male.

Yes, you say, but you really don't have a lot of choice here, either. Proper business attire is a matter of social convention. True. But you still have a choice. At some point you made that choice consciously. You may now be choosing your level of clothing (if not the specific tie or earrings) by habit or default, but you're still performing an act of free will.

I insist on this point (and have probably belabored it by now) because *becoming more conscious of the choices you make and learning to reclaim some of these choices is the very essence of effective time management.*

I'm not suggesting that you wear leather or cutoffs to business. I'm not suggesting that you give a great deal of conscious thought to whether you should brush your teeth, or what toothpaste you should use, or which hand you should hold the toothbrush in, or which quadrant of your mouth you should brush first. You should go right on performing such tasks by rote so long as your routine is effective for you. (And oh the havoc when, for example, you develop carpal tunnel syndrome in your dominant hand and have to try to learn to brush your teeth "wrong-handed.")

But if you're making *all* of your decisions by rote, you're probably not making the best decisions for yourself.

THE DILEMMA OF THE RINGING TELEPHONE

I'm going to ask you to spend a little time now to save a lot of time later. I want you to devote conscious thought to everyday choices you may not be thinking about now. The more uncomfortable you are with this exercise, the more potential it has to help you.

Imagine for a moment that you work in an office and that your office has a telephone (not too much of a stretch there). Imagine that the phone rings (again not a real feat of creative visioning, I suspect). Shall you answer it? Yes, you do have a choice (especially if you have voice mail or can let the call ring through to another phone), although most of us automatically snatch up a ringing phone. (Remember Pavlov and his salivating dogs? And we don't even get a biscuit as reward when we answer our bells!)

You usually have to make the decision to answer a ringing telephone without the most important piece of information, namely, who's on the other end. That's one reason why most of us answer the phone most of the time, even when it rings just as we sit down to dinner. It *could* be important, although it's more than likely somebody soliciting a donation or trying to sell you something.

Who's calling you right now? I could make it easy and tell you it's a financial planner making a cold call to solicit your business. But that wouldn't be much of a test case. Let's suppose, instead, that it's your significant other (hereafter referred to as the "SO"), the man or woman you share your life with, the single most important person to you on the face of the planet. Now do you want to answer the phone?

Well, sure, of course, except that...you *are* at work, and you're awfully busy, right in the middle of something important, on deadline, and, well, truth to tell, you wish you could know what the conversation was to be about before you committed to getting into it, right? Even caller-ID can't help you there.

But through the magic of the hypothetical case, I'm going to tell you exactly what your SO wants to talk to you about and then let you decide whether to pick up that phone or let it ring through. To avoid having to resort to he/she, (s)he, or other linguistic distractions, we'll let the SO be male in this case. Obviously, it works either way.

- **Case A**. Your SO just got off the phone after a long talk with his sister, Robyn, out in Oregon. She's having a terrible time with her oldest, Andrew, who just got expelled from school for getting caught with marijuana in his locker. Robyn's upset, and so's your SO, who doesn't know what he can do to help. He wants to talk to you about it.
- **Case B**. SO is calling to tell you that he seems to have lost all feeling on the left side of his face, and he feels as if he might pass out any minute.
- **Case C**. He wants to talk about your relationship. You had a fight last night, and you were both still upset when you went to work this morning. Some things need ironing out *right* now.
- **Case D**. Nothing special. He just wants to chat.

So, are you going to pick up that phone? It's your call (literally). I promise they'll be no repercussions; your SO will never know if you choose to duck him.

No question about Case B, right? You'll not only take the call, but you'll drop whatever you had going at work and race home to take him to the emergency room. Although it's a frightening and potentially horrible situation, it's also an easy decision to make.

Given the circumstances, Case D might be a fairly easy call, too. You'll talk later.

Case A is a little tougher. Of course you care about Robyn and Andrew and the whole unfolding soap opera out in Oregon. You care even more that your SO is upset and embroiled in a family problem. But there's certainly nothing you can do about it now (or probably ever, for that matter). And you do have that big meeting in 15 minutes to get ready for.

Do I hear that phone ringing through?

Case C is probably tougher yet. Your relationship with your SO is the most important thing in your life. But this isn't the time, the place, or the medium for a heavy discussion. Rehashing last night's argument now probably won't do any good and might even do some harm. And to tell the truth, you're at least a little angry that he'd call now, knowing how busy you are. And yet...

Maybe it's just as well we can't always know who's calling and what they're calling about.

IS IT IMPORTANT OR MERELY URGENT?

For sake of this discussion, let's define something as *important* to you if it touches on your core values, the basic motivations that guide your life. Something is *urgent,* on the other hand, if it demands your attention right now.

To be an effective time manager, you need to remember the distinction. You also need to remember that *everything that is important is not also necessarily urgent, and everything that is urgent is not necessarily important.*

Case B was an easy decision because the call was both important and urgent to you. The health and safety of a loved one is at stake (or at least seems to you to be, and there's no way you'd take a chance with something like that), and the situation demands immediate action.

So it is with anything in life that is both important and urgent. Although it may demand a great deal from us, it does not require any decision making.

Case C, the discussion about relationship, is also clearly quite important but may lack a sense of urgency (why *now*?) or even seem inappropriate (not *now*!).

Case A, with poor Robyn and Andy in Oregon, seems somewhat less important because it's one step removed from your SO, and perhaps even less urgent.

Case D carries with it the least sense of urgency.

And that cold-calling financial planner is neither important nor urgent, a real easy call to skip.

To really get a handle on this key distinction and to apply it meaningfully to your own life, you need to take a few minutes to think about your own activities and to sort them out.

THE FOUR CATEGORIES OF ALL LIFE'S ACTIVITIES

1. **Urgent and Important:** relates to your core values and needs attending to immediately
2. **Important but Not Urgent:** no sense of immediacy
3. **Urgent but Not Important:** doesn't touch core values
4. **Neither Important nor Urgent:** all the other stuff in life

Before reading on, list three or four activities in each category:

1. **Urgent and Important**

_____
_____
_____

2. **Important but Not Urgent**

_____
_____
_____

3. Urgent but Not Important

_____

_____

_____

4. Neither Important nor Urgent

_____

_____

_____

Here are a few samples to help you sort:

1. Urgent and Important
Call from day care—your child is throwing up
Big presentation to make in two hours
Car swerves in front of you

2. Important but Not Urgent
Exercising every day
Long-range financial planning
"Quality" time with family

3. Urgent but Not Important
Colleague needs to "talk with you right away about that
 Hansen deal"
Department meeting started four minutes ago
E-mail icon is blinking

4. Neither Important nor Urgent
Working a crossword puzzle
Catching up on office gossip
Reading the baseball box scores

Try to come up with at least three examples from your own
life in each category before reading on.

(Relax. I'm not going to recommend you stop working cross-word puzzles just because you put them in the "neither/nor" slot.)

Ready? Let's talk. There really is an important, maybe even urgent, point to all this. I want to focus on categories B and C, the "important but not urgent" and the "urgent but not important." Specifically, I want to suggest that you might be doing too much of C and not enough of B.

THE SECRET OF TIME MANAGEMENT REVEALED: WHY WE WASTE TIME ON TRIVIA AND DON'T SPEND ENOUGH TIME ON ESSENTIALS

Life is full of urgencies that really don't make any difference in the long run (or even in the short run, for that matter). Yes, you're four minutes late for that department meeting. But the department meeting is a fat waste of everybody's time (including the person running it), 90 minutes of plodding through announcements you could have read for yourself (or chosen to ignore).

Technology has increased our sense of urgency. An overnight letter cries for more immediate attention than something sent bulk rate or even first class, a fax outshouts an overnight letter, and e-mail outscreams them all. But the delivery system has no bearing on the importance of the content; that e-mail message may be no more important to you than the letter informing you that you "MAY ALREADY BE A WINNER!" in the big clearing-house sweepstakes.

We also have extremely important choices that don't carry with them any sense of urgency. Of course I should exercise regularly. I know it's good for me, mentally as well as physically. And I will. I absolutely will. Just not right now. Hey, I'm four minutes late for the department meeting.

Unless we take conscious control of our decision making, we'll tend to react to the urgent, even if it's relatively unimportant, and shun the important, unless it also carries a sense of urgency.

ASKING THE "WANT TO/HAVE TO" QUESTION

If all this business of dividing activities into four quadrants on an important/urgent grid seems like a lot of work—and it is—here's an easier way to begin to gain control of your daily life.

Again, you're going to need to develop a way to interrupt yourself several times a day. These interruptions can coincide with your mini-vacations, but they don't have to.

Simply stop what you're doing, take a breath, and ask yourself the following question:

"Is this what I want or need to be doing right now?"

You can, of course, modify the question to fit your own circumstances and your approach to life. (I've created this version by modifying the "Lakein Question" proposed by Alan Lakein in his 1973 book.) But be sure to touch on the three key elements:

Is this what I *want*
or *need*
to be doing *right now***?**

Note that it's "or," not "and." Obviously, a task can be a long way from what you'd really like to be doing and still be the thing you need to do.

If the answer to this question is "yes," go back to what you were doing. You will have affirmed your choice of activities and made your decision consciously, the key element in time management.

If you want or need to do it but not right now, put it off and do something with a higher degree of time sensitivity. That way, you'll avoid getting caught in deadline pressure later.

And if you neither want nor need to be doing it, now or ever—STOP!

It may seem amazing to you, but if you stick with the "want/need" question for 21 days (same satisfaction-guaranteed deal as with the vacations), you really will catch yourself doing things you can't justify doing on any grounds, and you'll find yourself shifting activities to better serve your needs.

This simple question can make a tremendous positive difference in the way you live.

KNOWING WHEN TIME ISN'T REALLY THE PROBLEM

To get the whole picture, we need to throw in one more element here:

Time management isn't always a matter of time at all.

Going to that department meeting and sitting in a passive stupor is neither important nor particularly pleasurable (unless you're a gifted daydreamer), but it is a lot *easier* than exercising.

Confronting the office deadline may be a lot easier for many of us than trying to iron out the kinks in our relationships. Often we will take the path of least resistance, especially if we can justify the choice on grounds other than ease. (I *have* to go to the meeting. It's my job.)

WHY YOU'LL NEVER BE ABLE TO "FIND" TIME

Time only needs "managing" because we don't seem to have enough time to do everything we want and need to do. In particular, we never seem able to "find time" for those important but not urgent activities.

Stop looking. You'll never *find* time. It isn't lost. You're living it. You have to consciously decide to live it in certain ways and not others. You have to *make* time by taking it away from one activity and giving it to another.

Conscientious and creative use of the to-do list can help here. If you want to exercise three times a week, if you need to do some long-range career and financial planning, if you care enough about another human being to want to nurture your relationship, you will schedule time for these things. Otherwise, you may not "get to them," and even if you do, you'll give them only your leftover time, when energy and focus are at their lowest.

You can make time for the important things in life by reducing time spent on the items in the last category, the "neither important nor urgent but just a lot of fun" area. But you shouldn't wipe this area out completely (even if you could) lest life become one long dental appointment. I often work two crossword puzzles a day. I used to justify the "waste" of time on the grounds that I am, after all, a writer. Words are my tools (as well as one of my passions). Crossword puzzles expand my vocabulary. Yeah, but truth to tell, I don't get much chance to use "adit" and "emu."

I've stopped trying to justify crossword puzzles. I work them because they're fun for me. That's enough. But when I need to make time for something else, I can cut them out.

You can also create time for yourself by slicing some of that "urgent but not important or even a lick of fun" stuff out. In the next two chapters, we'll work on ways to do just that.

Chapter 9

Who's Setting Your Agenda?

Learn How to Deal with the Time Snatchers

If anybody should be used to dealing with frantic folks, it's Bill.

Bill runs a lock and key shop near my office in downtown Madison and has for decades. In that time, thousands of folks have come to him in advanced stages of panic, locked out of the car with, of course, someplace to get to and no time to get there.

I'll admit to having had need of Bill's services a couple of times over the years, which is how I know about the sign he keeps next to the cash register on the counter, the one that announces: *"Your lack of planning does not constitute my emergency."*

Bill always gets them (okay, us) into our cars and on our way. He just doesn't get overly worked up about it.

How about you? Are you able to keep your head above water when other folks start making waves, or do you tend to catch the stress?

THE THREE LITTLE WORDS THAT CAN STEAL YOUR LIFE

The phone rings. You snatch it up before it can ring again.

"Are you busy?" the voice on the other end asks.

No! I'm just sitting here waiting for your phone call.

"Is this a good time to talk?"

There's never *a good time to talk!*

"Got a minute?"

I've got the same minute you do! What do you want to do with it?

Maybe you've been tempted to answer that way. But you're a conscientious and caring human being. You've learned that the customer is always right and that everybody, including your colleagues, are in one way or another your customers. So, instead of sarcasm or confrontation, you probably reply with something along the lines of, "Now's fine" or "Fire away" or "How may I help you?"

You've just signed a blank check. Now the caller gets to fill in the amount.

Those three innocent little words—"Got a minute?"—may be stealing your life, a few minutes at a time.

You can stop this time-erosion, and you can probably do it without hurting anybody's feelings. But hurt feelings or not, you need to take back control of your day, one (got a) minute at a time.

Let's take it from the top, from the moment somebody asks "Got a minute?" and see if we can work out a response someplace between, "Why, sure. Take all you want" and "Buzz off."

WHAT'S WRONG WITH "BUZZ OFF"?

It won't win you many friends—or customers—and influence people, of course. But beyond that, it may be inappropriate. You may want and need to have the conversation being offered you.

You have the right to decide.

That's the key to effective time management in a sentence. You have the right to decide how you spend your time, which is to say that you have the right to decide what you'll do this minute.

To make an intelligent decision, you need two critical pieces of information:

1. What does the caller want to talk about?
2. How much time does the caller want to talk about it?

When you have this information, you can decide *if* and, if so, how long to talk.

You have the right to ask.

In fact, you're not very smart if you don't.

There are lots of nice ways to do it. "How may I help you?" is a good one, since it focuses on the needs of the caller while eliciting the information you need. You can no doubt come up with several more to fit various situations. If you need to, write them down on a 6 x 9 card and keep them by the phone as a reminder and a cue card until you feel natural asking.

What about That Old Standby, "No"?

Is it ever okay simply to answer "Got a minute?" with "No"?

Of course. You get to decide, remember? If you really don't have a minute, "No" is the right as well as the accurate response.

You can follow it up by buying a little time ("Can I get back to you in about half an hour?") or by setting a specific time to talk. That way, you've asserted control over your schedule, which is to say, your life.

Note, though, that you've still signed a blank check; you've just postdated it. You still don't know what the conversation is to be about, and so you still don't know if you really want or need to have the conversation at all.

The Golden Rule Applied to the Three Little Words

If you practice effective responses to "Got a minute" long enough, you'll train some of your frequent interrupters to ask the right question in the first place, a question that will supply the information you need to answer it.

"I need about five minutes to discuss the Aarons project with you. Is this a good time?"

How about you? Is that the way you open a conversation, or are you just as guilty of the "Got a minute?" gaff as everyone else? Get in the practice of asking-as-you-would-be-asked. You'll get a lot better response.

But don't bother trying to teach the rest of the world to practice proper etiquette in the workplace. You're in charge of your life, not theirs. Besides, you probably won't convert anybody, and the effort won't make you very popular.

Consider this: it may be somebody else's *fault* for asking the wrong question, but it's your *responsibility* to take care of your own time.

RECOVERING FROM THE "TAKE A MEETING" SYNDROME

Somewhere along about the middle of the 1980s, folks stopped merely talking to each other. Whenever two or more are gathered in the workplace, it's a meeting.

We don't even just meet anymore. We "*have* a meeting" or "*take* a meeting." Raise the level of rhetoric and you raise the apparent stakes. "We need to have a meeting" somehow sounds much more important than "Got a minute?"

But summit conference or casual chat, you still have the same basic right to decide whether you want to have, or take, or do it.

We've all got itchy trigger fingers when it comes to our calendars and day planners. We hear the word "meeting" and practice our fast draw, whipping out those schedules.

"How about next Tuesday?"

"No good. I'm on the road."

"Wednesday?"

"What time?"

"2:00?"

"No good. I've got the Benson meeting."

"How long will that take?"

"At least until 4:00."

"How about then?"

"Can't do it. I have to be in Milwaukee by 5:00."

So it goes, until you find a common hole in the wall of appointments. You often have to extend the workday to do it.

"Okay. We'll meet at the donut shop at 4:00 a.m."

Before you wind up with crumbs on your chin at four in the morning, assert your right to ask questions and decide based on the answers you get before you commit. You need to know:

1. What's the subject matter?
2. Does it really require a meeting? (Maybe you can talk about it for two minutes right now and avoid having to meet later.)
3. Are you really the person to do the talking, now or later? (Actually, Phyllis is handling that account. You'd better talk to her.)

IT'S OKAY TO DRAW A BLANK

Where is it written that thou shall fill up every space on the calendar?

Even if you're doing a great job of asking for the information you need before committing to a meeting or even a conversation, you still may be winding up with a crammed calendar and a ton of work to lug home each night.

If so, it may be that you're just not comfortable saying "enough" until you've filled every space on the calendar. If so, repeat after me:

"It's okay to leave spaces."

Say it long enough and you'll believe it. Believe it and you'll do it. You don't have to give away every scrap of the day. Save some for yourself. If you aren't able to leave space blank, then box out time slots for yourself before someone else takes them.

What sorts of things go into those blank slots?

- Time to do the paperwork you've been doing nights and weekends
- Time to initiate instead of just reacting
- Time to think
- Time to read

Yes, thinking and reading are permissible in the workplace, even if you seldom see much of either going on. They're also two of the most important tasks you can perform to keep yourself effective and productive.

And one more activity you can use to fill that slot:

- Nothing

That's right. You really can schedule downtime. If an emergency butts its way into your carefully planned day, your downtime becomes the buffer zone, saving you from meltdown. And if nothing comes up, you can always find a good use for that time, right?

Here's another tip for effective calendar maintenance: get a calendar with wider time slots. If your planner gives you 10-minute increments during the business day, get one that gives you 15-minute slots. If you're using 15's, consider going to 30's. The fewer slots you have to fill, the less likely you'll be to overfill the day.

PLANNING BY THE COLORS INSTEAD OF THE NUMBERS

During a discussion on calendar management at a recent seminar, a fellow shared his method for controlling his calendar. Before deciding how he should be spending his time, he needed to create an accurate picture of how he was already spending it. Using felt marking pens, he went over several recent weeks in the day planner, color-coding various activities: yellow for meetings, for example, blue for presentations, red for prep time, and the like. When he stepped back to survey his masterpiece, he was struck by the dominance of yellow. He was simply spending too much time in meetings, which explained why he wasn't able to get to other activities.

Then he did something about it.

He color-coded the next several weeks of his life in advance, assigning set "yellow times" for meetings and also adequate blues and reds, to create what he judged to be a better balance. He scheduled meetings until he had filled all the yellow spaces. Then he stopped scheduling meetings. No more yellow; no more meetings.

I pass his system along to you, not only because you might want to try it, or modify it to your own circumstances, but also as an example of creative and bold time management.

WHO REALLY HAS A CLAIM ON YOUR TIME?

Let's go back to the scenario we developed in the last chapter. Suppose your SO calls and simply says, "We need to talk."

Can you hear yourself saying, "What do we need to talk about?" or "Are you sure I'm the one you need to talk to?" Neither can I.

Some people have a much higher priority in your life than do others. These folks also have a much stronger claim on your time. You've entered into relationships with your loved ones and friends, based on love, respect, and affection. You've entered into relationships with colleagues and bosses, too, based on a social contract.

The problem comes when we fail to discriminate, when we grant "most favored person" status to everyone who wants to "trade" with us. Do so, and you have less time for the ones who want, need, and deserve it.

Should the Squeaky Wheel Get All Your Grease?

If you fail to discriminate, you've ceded control of your life to others. You've also opened yourself to the possibility that you're neglecting important people in your life who aren't willing or able to be as demanding as some of the others.

Who are the silent people in your life who need your attention? Whose voice aren't you hearing in the clamor of the day-to-day? Name those friends whom you somehow just never get around to calling.

Make two lists. Label one "people I'm spending too much time with." Label the other "people I'm not spending enough time with." Start planning so that you see less of the people on list one and more of the people on list two.

WHEN YOU SHOULD CHUCK TIME MANAGEMENT: A MORALITY TALE

You can effectively control your interactions with others, reclaiming large portions of your life to live as you want to.

But that doesn't mean you always should. I need to tell you a story to illustrate the point. It's a true story, but I'll change the name of my co-star.

Right about the time I was mastering the time management technique of "getting rid of the time wasters," a former colleague, since retired, appeared at my office door one morning.

Thank you, Lord, I remember thinking. *You've sent me a test.*

Dave is surely one of the dearest men on earth, unfailingly kind, gentle, and conscientious. But he functions in a different time zone than I do. His sense of pace seems to be a lot slower than mine.

I figured he would provide a perfect opportunity to try out my new time management skills. I would manage Dave right out the door, and he wouldn't even know what hit him.

I immediately stood up. That's rule number one. I moved toward the door, cutting him off so that he couldn't violate my space. That way, I'd keep him standing, and, as any good time manager knows, bodies in motion tend to stay in motion, but once the butt hits the chair, you're stuck with a conversation.

I had all my best kiss-off sentences cued up and ready, stuff like, "I know how busy you are, so I'll let you go."

But something about his demeanor seemed to set off a quiet warning in my mind. "Don't do it," a voice seemed to whisper. "Don't brush him off." (I know. This sounds like Kevin Costner out in that cornfield in *Field of Dreams*. What can I say?) I heard myself inviting him in and asking him to sit down—even as my yammering conscious mind was screaming "No! Don't do it!" I was seeing my entire carefully planned day destroyed, appointments falling like dominoes.

Dave came uncharacteristically straight to the point. He had cancer. He needed an operation. He had told family but hadn't told anyone else at work. He was telling me because he considered me to be his friend. He was scared.

I expressed my concern and offered what comfort I could. Mostly, he just needed to tell someone, to let someone carry a crushingly heavy weight with him a little way. He had honored me by choosing me for the job.

A few minutes later, he stood up, gripped my hand in both of his, thanked me, and left. The whole exchange took no more than five minutes.

After he left, I was literally shaking, not only because of his news, but because of my awareness of how close I had come to giving him the bum's rush, leaving him alone with his fear.

There was nothing on my to-do list that day nearly as important as spending five minutes listening to Dave and caring about him. In fact, the encounter probably makes my short list of truly important encounters. We have to remain open to the moment and to the people who need us in life. It can't all be schedule and work.

The story has a happy ending. Dave came through the operation fine and is enjoying his retirement. He has moved away, and I haven't seen him in a long time. I miss him. If he shows up at my office door again, he'll get a warm welcome—no matter how busy I am.

Chapter 10

Is Your Staff Working Efficiently?

Seven Time Management Tips for Managers

Managing people takes time. It may take an inefficient or ineffective manager longer to plan, supervise, and evaluate someone else's work than to just do it herself.

The answer isn't to fire the staff. The answer is to manage them effectively. Here are seven time management tips that will help you do it.

1. Never Waste Their Time

Does the sight of one of your workers standing idle threaten you? If so, resist the temptation to assign busy work, just to keep them moving. You waste their time, of course, and you also waste your time, thinking up the work, explaining and supervising it, pretending to care about it when it's done.

You'll also be eroding their trust in you and your decisions. They know it's busy work!

Don't fill their time for them. Show them what needs doing. Show them how to do it. Make sure they have the tools they need. Then get out of the way.

2. Make Sure the Time Savers Are Really Saving Their Time

I recently conducted a time management seminar at a large Wisconsin company. As my host led me through the bullpen office area to the classroom, I noticed two folks standing by the fax machine, their bodies tensed with anticipation. As the machine started to whir, one reached out and actually tugged on the sheet of paper to make it come out faster.

What's wrong with this picture, two workers employed waiting for a fax to arrive?

The fax is supposed to save time, right? But we soon learn to fax material that could have (should have?) gone by good old pony express, and we put off writing the letter until it has to go by fax. That doesn't save time; it just increases pressure.

Somebody has to choose the fax, repair the fax, maintain the fax, and replace the fax with the new, improved, faster fax, bought with money somebody had to spend time to produce.

Have we "saved" time here? Not really.

I'm not advocating a retreat to the Stone Age. I don't even want to think about trying to write without a computer, research without the Internet, or handle phone calls without voice mail.

But these good slaves can make terrible masters, driving your staff to distraction with their bells and beeps and buzzers. Make sure the machines work for the people and not the other way around.

3. Separate the Important from the Merely Urgent for Your Staff

For your staff, as for yourself, you need to distinguish between truly important activities, those that serve the central mission, and the stuff that seems to demand immediate attention without really meriting it.

Do you and your staff ever engage in long-term planning, skills training, or needed conflict management? Or do these things get lost in the daily clamor?

You'll never "find" time to do these vital (but seldom urgent) activities with your staff. As a good manager, you must be sure to make the time.

Ask "Why?" for the phone calls and memos and faxes demanding your staff's immediate attention. Can you relieve some of the pressure and release your staffers for more important work?

4. Tell Them Why

"Why do I have to do this?"

If that question from a staffer feels like a threat to your authority, if you become defensive when you hear such a question, your staffers will learn to keep the questions to themselves.

But they'll still wonder.

They have the right and the need to know the purpose of their work. When you ask them to do something, give them a good reason.

You'll have a more motivated and more efficient workforce.

5. Allow Them Enough Time for the Task

Be realistic in your demands. Don't overstuff the staff. If you do, you'll get shoddy work. You might even get less work. Even a conscientious, willing worker does not perform well under unreasonable pressure.

6. Encourage Them to Do One Thing Well—at a Time

Watch your staff at work. Are they on the phone, jotting notes, eyeing the computer screen, all while trying to grab a fast sandwich?

Getting a lot done? Probably not. And they're probably not getting anything done well.

If your coworker is on the phone with a potential client, you want that worker's total attention on the task at hand, not thinking about the next project or the last project or the work that isn't getting done.

They'll work faster and better, with less need for clarification during or revision later.

This seventh and final tip is so important, it has been the subject of whole books.

7. Cut Down on Meeting Time!

Ask your staff to make a list of things they least like to do and chances are "go to a meeting" will rank right up there with "take work home over the weekend."

Most of us hate meetings, and with good reason. We avoid them if we can, resent them when we can't, and complain about them before, during, and after.

So, our first tip here ought to be obvious but apparently isn't: don't have a meeting if you don't have a good reason to meet.

That means never, right? Wrong. You really do need meetings. You can create a productive interaction that just doesn't occur with memos or e-mails or phone calls or one-on-one conversations. People get a better grasp of the whole operation. Names become faces, and faces become individuals. You can develop and maintain a sense of shared purpose and cooperation. In a meeting:

- Everyone hears the same thing at the same time, removing some (but, alas, not all) miscommunication.
- If people don't understand, they can ask for clarification.
- The speaker can use nonverbal clues (crossed arms, frowns, glazed eyes, eager nodding) to determine how people are responding to a proposal.
- Most important, when people interact, they create ideas that never would have occurred otherwise.

Schedule regular meetings. If you don't have a reason to meet, or if you have reasons not to meet, you can always cancel. Nobody ever complains about a canceled meeting, do they?

But every time you do have a meeting, make it worth their time and energy to be there.

Here's how.

1. Get ready.

You really have to know your stuff to explain it to others. Do your homework. Review your reason(s) for holding the meeting and the outcome(s) you want.

2. Get the meeting place ready.

Make sure you've got the flip chart and markers and overhead projector. How about visuals? Refreshments? Seating arrangements? Put them in rows facing front if you want them to sit quietly and listen (or fall asleep). Put them around a table if you expect them to take an active part in the discussion.

3. Get them ready.

Don't pass out copies of a thick report to start the meeting and then expect folks to read and react on the spot. Even the most willing worker won't be able to do a good job.

What do they need to know before the meeting? Get information to them at least two working days ahead of time. Sure, some won't read it. But many will, and they'll come prepared.

4. Get out an agenda.

Whatever else you send them before the meeting, be sure to circulate an agenda. Emphasize action items and spell out recommendations you plan to make. If they need to bring something with them (like their calendars, so you can plan yet another meeting), tell them now.

Be sure to indicate a reminder of the day, place, and time on the agenda.

5. Get rid of bad talk.

Don't let your meeting degenerate into personal attack or disintegrate into multiple sidebar discussions.

Here are a few ground rules other groups have found helpful:

- Use "I" statements in sharing your perceptions.
  Not: "This meeting is a stupid waste of time,"

But: "I feel like we're wasting our time here."

- Talk about issues, not personalities.
  Not: "Your idea is idiotic,"
  But: "I don't think this idea will work because . . ."

- Come prepared.
- Listen actively. Don't interrupt.
- Don't yell, pound the table, or curse.

You might not want or need these guidelines. Develop your own to work for your group.

Now what do we do?

So what are you going to do with all this time you've saved for your staff? You probably won't have trouble filling the time. But if you don't plan for it, existing jobs will simply expand to fill it.

Your final task as an effective time manager for your staff must be to consider how time really ought to be spent. Are there other important activities that haven't been getting done?

Before you spend all their time, though, consider giving a little time off as a reward for a job well done, ahead of schedule. You can't give them anything they'll appreciate more and that could motivate them better.

Chapter 11

Does Your "No" Really Mean "No"?

Learn How to Avoid Taking on Everybody Else's Burdens

"If you want something done," the adage goes, "ask a busy person."

Are you one of those busy people? Can you always be counted on to take on that additional job? You'll not only serve on the volunteer board, you'll chair it, take the meeting notes, edit the newsletter, and head up the recruitment subcommittee.

"I just don't know how you do it all," folks tell you.

Do you? Do you know *why* you do? And have you considered how much that extra work is costing you?

"I just don't have your energy," folks tell you, or "I can't ever seem to find the time"—right before they ask you to take on another job.

"We can always count on you!" they gush when you say "yes."

Your willingness to serve speaks well for you. You help because you believe in the cause and because you want to make your family, your workplace, and your community better places. You're a helper, a problem solver, a doer. You're community-minded, a team player, in sports parlance the "go-to person."

But you may be doing more than you should—for your own physical and mental health, for the well-being of your loved ones, and for your ability to be effective and efficient. To find out, examine your motives—all of them—for saying "yes" to each task. You may not like what you see.

THE NOT-SO-NICE REASONS FOR BEING SO NICE

1. Looking for Love in All the Right Causes. You do indeed earn the gratitude and approval of your peers when you shoulder their burdens. That approval and acceptance may in part be fueling your need to say "yes." Behind this desire may even lurk the fear that, if you don't work so hard, those around you will stop accepting you.

2. The Guilt Syndrome. "It's difficult to say 'no' when someone asks you to serve on a not-for-profit board, or chair a committee, or attend a fund-raiser for a very worthy cause," writes Jan Benson Wright, editor of *The Peoria Woman*. "When we decline, we are often inclined to shoulder a subsequent burden of guilt, because 'superwoman' failed to come through as expected."

3. The Myth of Indispensability. Rather than kindness, your effort may in part be motivated by arrogance. Perhaps you don't let others do the job because, deep down, you don't believe anyone else can do it or do it as well as you can. You've taken to heart the adage "If you want a job done right, do it yourself."

4. The Fear of Expendability. What if you didn't show up for work and nobody noticed? On some basic, subconscious level, you may be afraid that the moment you stop all your efforts, people will discover that they don't really need you at all.

Reasons three and four seem mutually exclusive. They're not. It's quite possible to feel both ways at the same time. Just as you can be in a "love/hate relationship," you can feel both indispensable and expendable.

If any of these motivations apply to you, *you may be saying "yes" because it's easier than saying "no."*

Understanding this about yourself is the first big step in summoning the courage to say "no."

Why All That "Yes" Sneaks Up on You

Glaucoma is a gradual hardening of the eyeball which, if left untreated, can cause blindness. It's an especially insidious disease; because the impairment is so gradual, the victim is often able to make subtle, unconscious adjustments to a slowly shrinking field of vision, becoming aware of the disease only when it's too late to treat it.

Making too many commitments can be like that, too.

"The problem with clutter in our lives, like clutter in our closets, is it arrives one piece at a time, never in basketfuls," Benson Wright notes. "It's not too difficult to refuse a huge, overwhelming load of additional responsibilities; it's tough, however, to decline 'just one more.'"

Add up all the extra tasks you perform, anything above and beyond what's required. Take your time; the effort will help you immensely to gain control over your life.

Here's the start of one person's list:

- Coach a Y basketball team
- Chair the workplace expectations committee at the office
- Coordinate United Way fund-raising in the department
- Serve as recording secretary for the church council
  and on and on . . .

These are all good things to do. Somebody should do them. But does it have to be *you* in every instance?

The items on your list are all good, worthy endeavors, too. You probably genuinely enjoy doing them. We tend to enjoy the things we do well and gravitate toward these tasks when we have a choice.

I'm a words person and often find myself as recording secretary and/or newsletter editor for just about every group or committee I serve on. My sister-in-law the CPA lands on a lot of budget and finance committees.

Time management would be a lot easier if there were obvious time wasters on your list and tasks you dreaded doing.

HE AIN'T HEAVY; HE'S MY COLLEAGUE

Your list of extra commitments may not be complete. You also need to figure in jobs you've taken on that rightfully belong to someone else—not some generic "other person" who could take over as committee chair if you stepped down, but the specific person whose job you've shouldered.

Connie hates to write up the required sales reports at the end of each day. She'd much rather be out in the field making more sales. You really don't mind the paperwork, and actually, you seem to have a flair for it. Yes, it's an extra hour or so at the office, but you really don't mind. . . .

Everyone is supposed to take a turn making the coffee at the office, but…Jeff makes it too strong. Sylvia never washes out the pot when it's empty. Nora leaves the machine on overnight. Gloria forgets when it's her turn. It's easier if you just go ahead and make the damned coffee!

A QUALITATIVE METHOD FOR COMPUTING THE TRUE COST OF YOUR COMMITMENTS

Got your list finished? (Don't worry. You can always add items as you think of them.) Now it's time to figure out what all that activity really costs you.

You probably have a good idea how much money you give to charitable causes. Many of us come up with a fairly precise number to report to Uncle Sam every April 15. This calculation enables you to make adjustments in next year's giving, bringing the level up or down to where you think it ought to be and redistributing funds according to your shifting awarenesses and priorities.

But most of us aren't nearly as conscious of how much time we're donating. This lack of awareness makes it much harder to change your level of involvement or redistribute your energies.

Put some numbers next to the items on your activity list. Estimate the amount of time you spend in a week, a month, or perhaps a year. You don't need mathematical precision here, but you do need honesty. Don't fudge.

When you add up those numbers, you begin to get a sense of how much your perpetual motion is costing you.

Money has value in terms of what it will buy for us (possessions, comfort, status, entertainment, relative freedom...). Same with time; we only truly appreciate its value in terms of what we can do with it.

What would you be doing if you weren't doing some of the activities on your list? We each carry around a lot of "if onlies . . .," things we say we'd do if only we could "find" the time. Make a list of your "if onlies . . .". Here are some examples:

If only I could find the time, I'd . . .

learn how to play golf
read the complete works of Mark Twain
get more sleep
master conversational Spanish
write my memoirs
have people over for a meal at least twice a month . . .

Perhaps you don't really want to *learn* Spanish; you simply wish you knew how to *speak* Spanish. The first is active; you'd really like to do the activity. The second is passive; you wish you already had the benefit of the activity. Even so, you may be willing to do the work to get the benefit. If so, leave the item on your list.

Take a good look at your list. It represents the true cost of your commitments. Line up the two lists, commitments on the left, yearnings on the right. Decide which activity on the commitment list you'll quit and which activity on the wish list you'll begin instead. Then do whatever it takes to make the switch.

ANOTHER SUBJECTIVE METHOD FOR TRIMMING THE ACTIVITY LIST

Go through your activity list twice more. On the first pass through, assign a number from 1 to 10 for each on the enjoyment scale, 10 being "highly pleasurable," and 1 being "pure drudgery." Then go through again, assigning a number from 1 to 10 on the importance scale, 10 being "crucial to the survival of the human race" (well, maybe not quite *that* important), 1 being "who really cares?"

Our hypothetical list of activities might look like this:

Activity	Enjoyment	Importance
Coach a Y basketball team	9	7
Chair the workplace expectations committee at the office	2	4
Coordinate United Way fund-raising in the department	1	8
Serve as recording secretary for the church council	5	5

Just looking at the numbers, it seems we've got ourselves a basketball coach here. If you give it a 9 on the enjoyment scale, you're probably also good at doing it. (That correlation doesn't always work, but it's an awfully strong indicator.) If you like it, you're good at it, *and* you think it's important, do it!

Want something to trim? I think it's time the workplace expectations committee found itself a new chair, don't you?

The United Way job is tougher to call. It may be extremely important, but you may not be the person to do it. The cold truth is, someone else who enjoys coordinating and fund-raising will probably do a much better job than you will.

THE "SOMETHING'S GOT TO GIVE" THEORY OF TIME MANAGEMENT

The next time someone asks you to take on a new activity . . .
The next time you find yourself starting to take over a task without even being asked . . .
The next time you're tempted for *any* reason to take on a new commitment . . .

Write the task on your commitment list and, next to it, write the specific activity you're going to give up to do it. Again, you need to be honest here; the time it took you to perform the old activity must equal the time required for the new one.

Here are some examples:

New Activity	Old Activity
Exercise on the treadmill (45 minutes every morning)	45 minutes of sleep
Chair the neighborhood recycling committee	Play with my kids on those Saturday mornings
Join a book discussion group (two-hour meeting each month, 10 hours to read the book)	Watch television (3 hours/week)

The first trade-off, exercise for sleep, may not be a good deal (although it's one I've made). Exercise is surely good for physical, mental, and emotional well-being. But so is sleep. Are you getting enough? Too much? Not enough (more likely)? We'll explore that question in detail in another chapter.

If you decide you need the sleep, that doesn't mean you can't also do the exercise. It means you have to figure out another trade.

The second trade-off is even more problematic. You may believe strongly that recycling is our last best chance to save the planet. But you also place high value on spending time with your kids, especially if you don't get to see them much during the week. Can you work another trade? You'd have to find a way that would also fit the kids' "schedules," of course. (Don't decide to give up watching *Saturday Night Live* to play with your four-year-old.)

Can't find a way to do the recycling without abandoning the kids? Then you might have to leave the recycling to somebody else.

The third example looks like a terrific swap. Instead of wasting time on mindless, godless television, you'll be exercising your critical skills and absorbing great literature. Maybe. But television and print are simply media of expression. The content surely has to factor into the equation. Are you giving up reruns of *The Gong Show* to read genuinely stimulating books? Go for it. But swapping *Masterpiece Theatre* for the complete works of Danielle Steele may not be a great deal. (I'm not saying it isn't. I neither watch *Masterpiece Theatre* nor read Danielle Steele.)

To do this right, you should figure in the quality of that two-hour group discussion, too. Are you having a good time in the company of stimulating conversationalists, or do you come home fuming over all those "stupid blockheads" in your reading group?

HEARTLESS? HUMBUG!

All this computing of relative worth may seem cold and calculating, and you do risk squeezing all the spontaneity out of life if you always draw up a list before you act. But the heartless figuring is in fact a way to heed your heart by giving more time to activities that support your core values.

You would never consciously choose to neglect your kids. But you might choose to spend less time with them by default, without realizing you were doing so, when you take on the socially worthy work of being your neighborhood recycling czar. Well-meaning resolutions to "make it up to them" might quiet your conscience, but it probably won't translate into actual time spent.

HOW TO SAY "NO"

All this figuring and calculating and deciding won't do you a bit of good if you aren't able to act on your decisions.

The moment is at hand. The out-going chair (desperate to find a replacement) has asked you to shoulder the burden. What do you say?

1. Beware the Automatic "Yes." You may have gotten into your time-trouble because you have a very hard time saying "no." But you've learned by bitter experience that it's *much* harder to get out of something later than to turn it down now.

2. Buy Time. Unless you're already *certain* of your response one way or the other, ask for time to think about it. This is both a reasonable and a truthful response. You really do want and need time to think about it (if not to pull out various lists and rating scales).

3. If the Answer Is "No," Say "No." Say it gracefully, but *say* it.

"I'm really flattered that you'd think of me. Thank you so much. But I'm going to have to turn the opportunity down."

And then shut up!

4. You Don't Have to Give a Reason. This may come as a shock. We're reasonable people. We like to think we're motivated by reason, and we want others to understand and agree with our rationale for our decisions. We want people to continue to think well of us. So we give reasons. And when we do, we open the issue to discussion.

"I'm just too busy right now."

"I know how busy you are. But actually this doesn't take very much time at all. And besides, you're so efficient and well-organized . . . ."

"I really don't think I'm the best choice for the job."

"You're just being modest. You're perfect for the job. Why, with your way with people and your ability to handle a meeting. . . ."

You'll lose this debate. You're arguing the negative position, often a much harder stance to support logically. You can be rationally talked out of something you feel strongly to be right and talked into something you know instinctively to be wrong for you.

If you "lose" (meaning you fail to get them to say "You're right. Sorry I asked"), you've got two alternatives, neither of them good. You can acquiesce and agree to take on the task. Or you can stick to your guns and continue to say "No," leaving both of you much more upset than necessary.

Decide, based on your informed understanding of your motives and the true costs and benefits of the activity. Then stick to your decision! You'll find yourself with a great deal more conscious control of your life.

Chapter 12

Are All Your Gadgets Really Saving You Time?

Learn How to Manage the Machines

The moment Alexander Graham Bell created the telephone, he used it to summon his assistant from the next room.

We've been dancing to the telephone's tune ever since.

They're everywhere. Cellular phones have been showing up on the ski slopes of Vail, Colorado. Vending machines in California will sell you a phone. Commercial airlines and rental cars often come equipped with them. Ringing phones and their advance scout, the beeper, have startled audiences at the theater and the opera, occasionally prompting fist fights. The ringing of the phone has become as toxic to some restaurant patrons as second-hand smoke.

Can cellular phone implants at birth be far behind?

The last three area codes in North America have been used up to provide relief for overnumbered regions in Philadelphia, Michigan, and North Carolina.

Although the average charge for cellular phone use has dropped, revenues rose almost 40 percent in 1996, to about $7.8 billion.

We have become a bell-bedeviled nation.

We can speed dial and speed redial. We've got call forwarding, call blocking, and call waiting.

Should you somehow manage to elude an incoming call, despite all this technological wizardry, your voice mail will preserve every word of the message and demand that you listen to it and in some way respond to it the moment you get back in range.

More and more now, your own calls to businesses involve contact with a recorded or a digitally fabricated voice.

> If you wish to receive information about arrivals and departures, press 1.
>
> If you wish to make reservations, press 2.
>
> If you wish to talk to a customer service representative, good luck . . .

I'm not advocating that we toss the technology out the window and go back to tin cans with strings. I love being able to punch in my electric meter reading on my digital phone, and I'm actually learning to use voice mail effectively to screen and organize my calls.

I am advocating that you take a good look at the technology in your life to determine what's helping and what's getting in your way.

We begin, of course, with the money spent on equipment and training, and the time it takes to earn that money. If you're an early adaptor, among the first to embrace the new technology, you get a jump on the competition, but you also pay more, make more mistakes, and endure while the manufacturer perfects the process.

But as with so many things in life, it isn't the initial cost so much as the upkeep.

TALLYING THE TRUE COST OF TECHNOLOGY IN TERMS OF TIME

The Time It Takes to Select It

I used to eat at a little diner called "The Red and White." Ruthie handled the grill while Red served up the burgers. The line was always four or five deep behind each of the nine stools, but the regulars found the food and the floor show worth the wait. When your turn at the counter finally came, Red would slap down a sheet of waxed paper and the plastic holder and paper cup for your water and bark out "With or without?"

That was the only choice. You took your burger with a thick slab of raw red onion, or you took it without the onion. No menu, no "California burgers," no well done or medium rare. You got it the way Ruthie grilled it, "with or without."

I took mine "with," hunkered down at the counter, enjoyed my burger and coffee, and listened to Red and Ruthie's inspired bickering.

Buying a telephone used to be like that. The telephone was a squatty box with a dial on its sloped face. You got it in black or white.

Now we've got choices. Oh, do we have choices! Phones come in every imaginable size and shape, let alone color, and you need a consultant to determine the right package of services and options for your business.

Choice is good. I like choice. But choice takes time.

When you figure the true cost of something like a telephone (or a computer or fax or any other modern wonder), don't just add up the dollars they cost. Count in buying time.

The Time It Takes to Learn How to Use It

By now the user manuals which accompany our new toys have become legendary for their incomprehensibility. Most seem to have been written either by the person who programmed the machine (and who thus has no idea why you can't automatically figure out how to use it) or by someone who has never used it and who has no intention of ever trying to use it. The prose then seems to have been poorly translated from a language having nothing in common with English.

Count your time spent crawling up the slippery slope of the learning curve, along with time blown making mistakes. (Admit it, now. How many pages of text did you lose into the ether while trying to master your first word processing program?)

The Time It Takes to Get It Fixed

You do in time learn (some of us much faster than others, of course). You and your machine bond and become an efficient team. Then one horrible morning, you flip the switch, and nothing happens. Or worse, lots of things start happening, all of them bad. Bells ring, error messages blink like the lights of the police car you've just noticed in your rearview mirror, and your beloved program icons blink off like dying stars.

Your partner has gone on strike.

You've got to either fix it yourself—or pay someone else to fix it. Count repair time/money into the true cost, too.

Downtime

As you master the technology, you become dependent on it. Who would go back to the old typewriter after learning how to compose and edit text on the computer? (Could you even *find* a typewriter now, let alone someone to repair it?) So when the computer goes down, word processing and number crunching stop.

Just as you must calculate employee sick time as part of the cost of doing business, you now must figure for the times when the computer is sick, too.

So, along with the sticker price, your checklist for computing the true cost of technology must include:

- Buying time
- Learning time
- Maintenance time
- Downtime

You may not need to compute specific figures for these factors. Simply being aware of them will give you a more realistic picture and, with it, a chance to take better care of your time. But you probably could make fairly accurate estimates if you needed to, since "time" by its very definition is a tangible unit of measurement.

Then you also need to try to factor in the human elements.

FACING UP TO THE ANNOYANCE FACTOR

Time was, when I tried to call you on the phone at your place of business, I either got you or I didn't. I got to talk to a human (you or somebody who worked with you) or I got a busy signal. Now I most often wind up in the telephone twilight zone, as your mechanical surrogate invites me to talk to a machine.

I've pretty much gotten used to that. In fact, I've gotten to like it. It's like having your own 15-second radio show for an audience of one; I always try to have some good material ready.

But some folks don't like talking to machines. Some feel nervous about having their voices recorded. Some will hang up without leaving a message. Some won't bother to call back.

Hard to calculate the cost of the "tick-off factor," but it's there.

Personally, I'd much rather talk to your machine than get you for a breathless few seconds, only to have you dump me the moment you find out you've got another call coming in.

You're not fooling anybody, you know. I can hear that little thunk on the line. So when you say "Can you hold on for just a second?" I know to add what you didn't say: "I've got somebody else on the line who may be a hell of a lot more important than you."

How many people have you ticked off this week with call waiting?

CAN YOU RETAIN "HIGH TOUCH" IN THE AGE OF TECHNOLOGY?

Why would anybody shop at a neighborhood grocery store?

They charge more, they have less selection, and the shelves are so close together you can barely get your body, let alone a cart, down the aisle.

Habit and proximity play a role. But the primary advantage the little guy maintains over the chain store is personal service, the high-touch factor.

The fellow at the cash register greets you by name. He asks after your family, remembers that your daughter has a band recital coming up, forgets that your son is flunking math. He has saved a copy of your favorite magazine for you, and he'll trust you until next time if you come up a few dollars short. If the milk you bought has already gone bad by the time you get it home, he'll replace it for you, no questions asked.

Most of us don't shop at the corner grocery anymore, but we still yearn for a place where "everybody knows your name." Large organizations try to re-create the personal touch of the small business, as when the big bank promises that you'll be a name, not a number, to its tellers.

Some huge corporations have managed to retain the personal touch. Perhaps lured by the folksy, conversational copy in its "magalog," you might call Lands' End, the giant direct mail merchandiser based in Dodgeville, Wisconsin. If you do, you'll speak to a friendly, knowledgeable human being, not a machine. If you aren't satisfied with the merchandise you receive, you can return it for any reason—or no reason—even if you've had it monogrammed, for a full refund. Technology and high touch aren't mutually exclusive.

THE PARADOX OF "IMPERSONAL COMMUNICATION"

But the fact remains, the more gadgets we place between ourselves and our clients, customers, and colleagues, the more impersonal our interactions become.

In one sense e-mail combines the best of written and oral communication. We can edit messages before we send them, and we can reread and save the messages we receive. At the same time, e-mail communication is almost instantaneous, and we can capture some of the spontaneity and give-and-take of a telephone conversation. I've discovered that I can communicate better with some people via e-mail than by any other medium.

But there's no getting around the fact that e-mail is filtered and can be anonymous. We've introduced "netiquette" to preserve civility on-line and "emoticons" to communicate mood, but it's still words on a screen. "Flaming" (INSULTING MESSAGES, USUALLY IN ALL CAPS), "spamming" (a flood of unwanted messages), even stalking occur on-line, and we've already had our first report of a marriage arranged on-line gone sadly awry when the "groom" turned out to be a woman.

There really is nothing as immediate and effective as face-to-face communication. Although our amazing technology has in one sense brought us closer together in terms of speed and accessibility, it has also driven us apart in terms of actual human contact.

TECHNOLOGY AS WASTE OF TIME

We need to look at one more factor on the negative side of the time/technology equation, the most obvious and yet least-talked-about element: on-line goofing off. Technology in general and the computer in particular have made it much easier to play while appearing to work.

E-mailing with a friend looks the same as writing the quarterly report. Downloading pictures from the *Penthouse* web site involves the same process as doing product research on the net.

Even well-meaning, conscientious workers who wouldn't think of playing "Tri-Peaks" on company time may be creating occasions to use e-mail and cruise the net, simply because they are enjoyable activities.

WHAT HAS HAPPENED TO ALL THE TIME YOU'VE "SAVED"?

One of the arguments for quitting smoking—though far from the most compelling one, in my view—is the financial one: think of all the money you'll save.

Suppose you used to smoke a pack a day, but at the urging of loved ones and your own increasing awareness of the health risks involved, you quit a year ago. At $2 a pack, you will have saved $730.

So, where's the money?

Unless you took that $2 a day, stuck it in a sock, and hid it under the mattress, you don't actually have that $730 now, and you probably can't account for how you spent it.

I did smoke a pack of cigarettes a day in my reckless youth. I quit almost 30 years ago (and yes, I still crave a cigarette now and again). Cigarettes didn't cost nearly as much back when I was puffing, but even at an average of a buck a pack, I should have saved close to $11,000 by not smoking all that time. But I can't put my hands on the cash now.

If you add up all the negatives involved in acquiring technology and still reckon that your technology is in fact saving time for you, then you need to ask yourself one more important question: where is all that time you saved?

Technology was supposed to lead us into the Age of Leisure. (The computer was supposed to create the "paperless office," too. Wrong on both counts.) There are at least three reasons why technology may not actually be saving you time in any useful sense:

1. The Fallacy of Increased Expectations. Instead of decreasing the amount of time we take to process a report, the computer may have increased our expectations of how long the report should be, how many graphics it should contain, and how many times it should be edited. If a longer, more heavily edited and lavishly illustrated report is in fact more useful, the company has benefited. But it may simply be a fatter report requiring a great deal more effort to produce.

2. The Last-Minute Syndrome. When we knew we'd need at least two days to send a report by surface mail, we set our deadlines accordingly. The advent of overnight mail allowed us to push that deadline back a day. The fax allowed us to wait until the next-to-last minute. E-mail lets us transmit the material as we write it (if we're foolish enough to do it). None of this has saved us any time. It has simply allowed us to put tasks off longer. (Unless we're careful, it will also damage the quality of our written communication.)

3. The "If You Build It They Will Come" Phenomenon. Main Street used to run right through the middle of town. As traffic increased, we built a by-pass to ease congestion. The by-pass then got congested, and so we built a by-pass for the by-pass. You can read some towns' histories in the strata of their by-passes, like looking at layers of rock in the wall of the Grand Canyon. Traffic seems to increase in direct proportion to the number and size of the roads we build to accommodate it.

In the same way, communication may be expanding to fill the channels we've created for it.

RETAKING CONTROL OF THE TECHNOLOGY

Bill Henderson has chosen to opt out of the Communications Revolution.

Henderson is the founder of the Pushcart Press, one of the best independent publishers in America. More recently, he's also the guiding light behind the Lead Pencil Society, a growing group dedicated to the principle that simple ways are best. Henderson's patron saint is Henry David Thoreau, the son of a pencil maker and the author of the famous dictum: "Simplify, simplify."

You don't have to forsake all technology. (I believe that even Henderson still uses modern printing processes to produce his excellent yearly anthology of small press literature, *The Pushcart Prize*.) But you do need to make sure that you are using the technology and that it's not the other way around.

To regain control of the gadgets, begin with this simple premise:

Just because you can doesn't mean you have to.

Through the miracle of modern technology, you can be in constant touch with your associates, and you can grant them 24-hour access to you. But do you really *want* to? Constant access means constant interruption, and that may not be conducive to efficiency (or sanity).

Three Ways to Make Good Decisions about Technology

1. Get Only What You Need. During the recent global insanity known as the Arms Race, the former USSR and the United States stockpiled ever greater quantities of nuclear armaments, each Superpower developing the capacity to wipe out the entire world several times over. This would seem to make no sense unless viewed as a competition. There is no "enough" or "right amount"; we simply need to be sure we have *more*.

Are you engaged in a technological "RAM Race" with the competition? If so, know that you can never win. No matter what you get, someone else will have bigger, better, newer. About the time your staff becomes proficient on one software, its producer will introduce an upgrade making yours "obsolete."

Assess your needs. Use that assessment to obtain only the equipment and training you need, planning for orderly growth and development.

2. Learn Only What You Need to Know. I know how to drive a car. I know how to put gasoline, oil, and windshield wiper fluid in my car (although my wife is much better at the latter task). I know the phone number and address of a reliable, honest mechanic.

I do not, however, understand how the internal combustion engine works (despite having read several lucid explanations).

I also don't really understand how computers work. To me they are marvelous and magical. I know several word processing programs, can speak Mac and Windows, and can lay out a decent publication in PageMaker. I've learned new skills as I've needed them to do my work.

But I have no intention of mastering programming, just as I'll likely go to my grave still ignorant of that marvelous hunk of machine under the hood of my car.

3. Create Communication-Free Zones. Do you have to answer a ringing phone?

It's nearly impossible for some of us not to, but letting the phone ring may be the first big step in reestablishing control over the technology.

Set reasonable limits for yourself, and clear space of all interruptions. Here are three ways to do it. You'll think of others.

- Establish a "No Communications" Hour. I'm at my best early in the workday. I try to reserve an early-morning hour for writing and thinking, with no phone calls, no e-mail, and no faxes. The "No Communications" Hour can, of course, be longer or shorter than an hour, can be company-wide or confined to certain departments or individuals, can be the same time for everyone or can occur at different times.
- Bunch Your Communications. Return e-mails and phone messages during one or two scheduled periods each day. Make exceptions, if any, only for priority callers.
- Signal Your Intentions. When you leave a message for someone to get back to you, tell them when you'd like to be contacted. This allows you some control of incoming communications, and it also helps the caller avoid wasting time calling when you aren't accepting calls.

Our technology has brought us amazing access to information. It has also opened us to a bewildering flood of useless information and misinformation. In the next chapter, we'll look at ways to sift through the data—without spending all day doing it.

Chapter 13

Do You Know So Much You Don't Know Anything?

Learn How to Combat Information Overload

We live in the Information Age. No matter who you are or where you live, you're now as close as a computer and a telephone line to a virtual sea of numbers, words, and pictures on every possible subject.

You've got access, pal.

The Internet has been hailed as the Second Coming of Gutenberg, the great democratizer of knowledge, our salvation from all ignorance.

It has also been demonized as a smut peddler, a substitute for life, a potential addiction, and the final destroyer of the printed page.

It's just a tool, as morally neutral as a blank sheet of paper and a pencil. Like any tool, it can be used for a variety of motives, and it can help you or hurt you, depending on how you use or misuse it.

The good news: Just about anybody can create their very own Home Page.

The bad news: Just about everybody *has* created their very own Home Page.

Good news: Everything you could possibly want or need to know is on-line.

Bad news: Tons of stuff you have no possible interest in is also on-line.

Good news: It's all there.

Bad news: You have to sort through it all, and a lot of the "information" is wrong.

This description of the Internet as "Superhighway" circulated via e-mail a while back:

"A highway hundreds of lanes wide. Most with pitfalls or pot-holes. Privately operated bridges and overpasses. No highway patrol. A couple of rent-a-cops on bicycles with broken whistles. Five-hundred-member vigilante posses with nuclear weapons. A minimum of 237 on-ramps at every intersection. No signs. Want to get to Ensenada? Holler out the window at a passing truck to ask directions."

Your job is to find the good stuff while avoiding the bad, the irrelevant, the inane, and, most important, the downright wrong. You can get lost out there, and you can waste a ton of time trying to find your way back.

You can also emerge looking like a total idiot. Just ask Pierre Salinger, former press secretary to President John F. Kennedy, who went public with "conclusive proof" that a U.S. Navy missile had shot down TWA Flight 800, "proof" he and about a zillion other webheads had gotten from the net and which was totally bogus.

The net has already spawned its very own psychological syndrome, information anxiety, defined as "the widening difference between what you think you should understand and what you can understand." If it's all out there, and if access to it is so easy, then shouldn't I know more—and more and more?

Relax. Let's put all this net nonsense in proper perspective.

FOUR FUNDAMENTAL TRUTHS ABOUT THE INTERNET

1. Most People Aren't on It Yet

As part of the 1994 Republican Contract with America, House Speaker Newt Gingrich promised a computer, not a chicken, in every pot. Fact is, though, lots of folks still don't have computers, and many of those who do have them use them as electronic toys, not reference libraries.

Only 18 percent of mutual fund shareholders have Internet access, and only 28 percent of them have gone on-line to check mutual fund sites, according to a recent study sponsored by American Century Investments and reported in the *New York Times*.

Mutual fund shareholders are hardly ghetto dwellers, and their ranks undoubtedly include some of the "early adapters" who try out the new technology before the rest of us become convinced. And yet 82 percent of them don't even have access to the net, and 72 percent of them haven't borrowed somebody else's computer or used the desk terminal at work to check up on their money.

Access will, of course, continue to rise, but predictions of the world web community are as yet premature.

2. The Net Won't Wipe Out Other Media

New media don't destroy old ones. They cause the old ones to change.

Case in point: the advent of television was supposed to run radio right off the airwaves. All the pundits said so. Radio had been our constant companion, keeping us company (Don McNeil, Arthur Godfrey, Art Linkletter), educating and informing us, and telling us stories, endless stories ("Just Plain" Bill, Helen Trent, Mary Noble, Ma Perkins).

Radio didn't die when television took over as our main source of news and information, our national storyteller, and our "talking night light" (as one wag dubbed it). It changed—from broadcasting to "narrowcasting," with focused formats like easy listening (or "music of our lives"), oldies, hard rock, soft rock, all talk, and all news. Radio has become interactive now. We call Bruce for financial advice, Dr. Joy and Dr. Laura for love advice, Dr. Dean for medical advice. We go to Art for UFO and alien-invasion updates and to Rush for a big swig of conservative philosophy and media bashing.

Radio has survived and thrived by learning to serve different needs.

3. You Won't Become a Net Junkie

Heroin is addictive. Nicotine is addictive. Caffeine is addictive. Alcohol is addictive, at least for people who are genetically susceptible to alcoholism.

The net is not addictive. There's no such thing as "net addiction."

It may absorb *way* too much of your time, especially at first. For some it may supplement and perhaps even replace face-to-face human contact, as "virtual relationships" become a fact of modern life. For some it has no doubt become a way to escape "real life" or a means of manifesting inherent compulsivity.

But so far as we know, it doesn't alter brain chemistry or increase the number of neuro-receivers. "Net withdrawal," to the extent that it exists, is psychological, not physical.

And the compulsive and evasive will always find means of escape, perhaps "playing solitaire 'til dawn with a deck of 51," as the old Statler Brothers classic "Flowers on the Wall," puts it.

4. Information Is Not Wisdom

It's not even knowledge. It's just information.

YOU ARE THE QUALITY CONTROL

The net is disorderly at best and total chaos for the beginner (or "newbie" in computer slang). It's awfully hard to find your way.

The computer gives you access to just about everything, but it doesn't synthesize and sift. If you haven't been trained to abstract, synthesize, and summarize, this can be an enormous—and time-consuming—challenge.

And finally, you must distinguish the wheat from the chaff, useful information from nonsense, "true facts" from downright fabrication. If Pierre Salinger couldn't do it, how can you?

FIVE WAYS TO VERIFY INFORMATION ON THE NET

1. Check the Date
I always check the "best if purchased before" date on the carton of milk before putting it into my cart. Information has a shelf life and can spoil, too. Check to see when the site was last updated.

2. Consider the Source
Don't unplug your skepticism when you plug into the net. Boot up your bunk detector when you log on. Always ask the fundamental question: "Says who?"

Notoriety is not a substitute for knowledge, and "credibility" does not equal veracity. Even well-known and widely acknowledged sources can be flat-out wrong. (Just ask radio doctor Dean Edell how he feels about venerable newscaster Paul Harvey as a source of medical information.)

3. Track Down the Ultimate Source
By the time you get your information on-line, it may have passed through many computers, been filtered by many minds. What's the initial source of the information? Pay attention to the citation, the "according to." Sometimes you have to hunt to find it, lost in the linkage garble that tells you where messages came from.

If you can't find the primary source, ask.

If nobody will tell you where the stuff came from, be especially suspicious.

This isn't just a problem for on-line information, of course. "Usually reliable" print sources can be just as wrong. The venerable *Atlanta Journal-Constitution* assured the nation that Richard Jewell was the Olympic Bomber. *The San Jose Mercury News* ran a three-part series linking CIA-backed contras in Nicaragua to crack dealers in Los Angeles.

When a book titled *Our Stolen Future*, carrying an introduction from Vice President Al Gore, broke the scoop that "synthetic hormones" in the environment were causing severe declines in sperm counts, media picked up the story of the threat to the human race. Other researchers immediately challenged the conclusions, but they didn't get near the press.

Where did these revelations come from before the media picked them up?

4. Separate Fact Statements from Opinion Statements

A fact statement can be verified. If someone tells you that it's raining, you can look out the window to determine for yourself if moisture is indeed falling.

A fact statement can be true or false. It may, in fact, *not* be raining, in which case "it's raining" is a false statement of fact, but it's still a statement of fact because you can prove or disprove it.

A false fact statement may be innocent ("Gee, I really thought it was raining," or "Gosh, it was raining a minute ago") or intended to deceive.

"The weather stinks" is an opinion statement. You can determine the presence or absence of precipitation, but you can't prove that the weather stinks. Some folks love the rain.

Even "it's raining" may be subject to interpretation, of course. One person's rain is another person's drizzle or heavy mist or thick dew. There are few absolutes in this life.

But you can and must separate fact statements from opinion statements and evaluate them accordingly as you sift and winnow your way through the bewildering array of "info-bites" on-line.

5. Cross-Check

"If your mother says she loves you, get a second source."

This bit of cynical wisdom drives every good reporter to verify fact statements for accuracy by getting a second and perhaps a third source.

If sources conflict, get a tie-breaker, or simply note that you've got conflicting "facts" to deal with and withhold judgment before basing your conclusions on such a shaky foundation.

THREE WAYS TO AVOID DROWNING IN ALL THAT INFORMATION

1. Give Yourself Permission Not to Know Everything about Everything

You can now get current weather reports for anywhere on earth, determine the precise distance between most any two towns in America (along with their latitude and longitude and the compass setting to get from one to another), and learn the current state of Hillary Clinton's hair.

You can. That doesn't mean you should. And it certainly doesn't mean you have to.

We've heard our government officials spout nonsense about "credible deniability" (a euphemism for "I lied"). While I reject that notion, I embrace the concept of "permissible ignorance." I don't have to keep track of Elizabeth Taylor's husbands, and neither do you.

Figure out what you really want and need to know. Again, it may be the difference between knowing how to drive and knowing how to build an internal combustion engine. How much is enough?

2. Rip, Read, and Recycle

Practice skimming for main ideas and scanning for specific information. Learn to read titles, abstracts, summaries, subtitles, illustration captions, boldface text, and "pull quotes" to glean main ideas in a hurry. It works for print, and it works on the net, too (although learning how to skim on a screen is a new skill and requires practice).

Don't print it out unless you're sure you need it on paper. If you create a piece of paper now, you're going to have to file it, route it, pitch it, or recycle it later.

3. Create a Reading File for Airports, Busses, and Waiting Rooms

You don't need to read it right this minute. Print it out and put it in your "to-read" folder. This saves you the reading time now and enables you to put waiting time to good use later.

But if you do print it out, don't keep it any longer than you need to. Clutter robs you of the time it takes to move it, clean it, and wade through it to find what you need.

MARK YOUR SOURCES AND STICK WITH THEM

Addresses on the net tend to be rather long and somewhat complicated, stuff like: http://www.marshallcook.com/~timemanagement/guru/reallysmartguy_online.

You can spend a lot of time just typing in addresses (not to mention the time lost when you misplace a ~ or slant your \ the wrong way, so you have to start all over again).

On my program, when I find a site I like, I can set a "bookmark." Next time I want to visit that site, I can simply scroll down my list of bookmarks and click on the one I want. Your program has something similar. Use it!

But be sure to go through your bookmarks regularly to purge the ones you're no longer using, lest your tour through your site list become almost as cumbersome and time-consuming as typing in addresses.

Here are a few of my favorite sites:

- "My virtual reference desk" includes "virtual facts on file," with dictionaries, a thesaurus, atlases, encyclopedias, a who's who, even genealogical information.

- "Newslink" plugs you in to breaking news and even allows you to construct your own personal morning newspaper by letting you set up a template of subject areas you want to skim.
- "Switchboard" is a national electronic telephone directory. If someone has a listed number, you can find them on switchboard. As with most sources, the more you know, the easier it is to find what you want. Try typing in "Smith" and see how many matches you get. But type in "Smith, Jonathan, Dothan, Alabama" and you'll limit your search considerably.
- Many publications now have an on-line news service. I like the *New York Times* but also nibble at my old hometown newspaper, the *San Francisco Chronicle*, as well as many others. I must admit, however, that I still prefer the print version, but then, I was raised that way.
- "Baseball links." Okay. I didn't say I stuck to business all the time.
- Excellent on-line magazines include *Salon*, *Slate*, and *Vagabond*. As I write this, all of these sources are free once you have access to the Internet. *Slate* was going to start charging for access to its on-line material but backed off.

Here are a few of the facts I've found fast for recent writing projects:

- Who really first said "Go West, young man" (it wasn't Horace Greeley)
- The distance from Livingston, Montana, to Guntersville, Alabama
- The percentage of Americans who say they believe in God
- The name of the group that recorded the song "Mairzy Doats"
- The source of prizefighter Jack Dempsey's nickname, "The Manassa Mauler"

From my computer in Madison, Wisconsin, I was able to access a complete biography, a personal website, and a flood of news clips on California Assemblyman John Vasconcellos, all in a matter of minutes, without getting out of my chair.

I'm convinced that the net can open us up to the world without absorbing all our time if we use it wisely.

AN ODE TO THE JOYS OF AIMLESS BROWSING

If you're the kind of person who can't look up a word in the dictionary without getting sidetracked reading about a dozen other words, you're certainly a prime candidate for time management. You're also my kind of person.

I've learned some of the best stuff while looking for something else.

You want to make efficient and effective use of the web. You don't want to let it suck you in and waste your time. But browsing can be educational as well as joyful. Reading "outside your field" is one of the best ways to expand your scope, consider new points of view, and give yourself more of the raw materials you need to have new ideas and create solutions.

Schedule time for "surfing," especially when you're new to the net.

Chapter 14

Speed Writing:

Learn How to Get It Down on Paper or Up on the Screen ASAP

I can proudly say that I'm a professional writer. I make my living writing books and articles and coaching other people to do the same.

The term may not appear in your job description, but I'll bet you're a professional writer, too.

You may not write books—or even annual reports or business plans. But you probably write memos, letters, work orders, directions, equipment orders, job evaluations, responses to job evaluations, resumes, and a lot of other excursions into putting marks on paper or screen so they'll make sense—the sense you intend—for a reader.

But unlike me and other folks who carry "writer" as their primary job designation, you do a lot of other things every day. You can't afford to spend a lot of time with writing. You also can't afford the time it takes to do it over and to clear up the confusion and misunderstandings that poor written communication engenders.

FIVE TIPS FOR WRITING IT RIGHT—AND FAST—THE FIRST TIME

1. Keep It Short and Simple

The Ten Commandments requires fewer than 300 words, and Abe Lincoln only needed 271 for the Gettysburg Address. You ought to be able to get your thoughts down in a couple of hundred words, too, saving your time and the reader's.

Cut out each and every word that you don't really, really, really need. Don't even say "in order to" if a simple "to" will do.

Make your words easy to read by highlighting the main ideas. You can emphasize an idea by

- putting it first;
- using underlining, boldface, or larger type;
- breaking a list out from paragraph form with bullets (as I'm doing now);
- breaking thoughts into separate sections with subtitles.

Be sure to emphasize any action you've taken that affects your coworkers and any response you need from them.

Eschew obfuscation. Pardon me. I mean keep it simple and clear.

In Jeff MacNelly's great comic strip "Shoe," the boss tells the hapless employee, "We're taking this disagreement to alternative dispute resolution."

Huh?

It's "my way or the highway," the boss explains.

Ah, that we understand.

Plain talk is always best. Simple, direct language takes less time to compose and less time to understand.

The employment of ponderous polysyllables is pusillanimous.

Huh?

Only a coward hides behind big words.

Ah.

2. Get Off to a Flying Start

Formal outlines are a waste of time. If you need to organize your thoughts before you write, create a bubble outline. Identify your subject and write it in the center of a sheet of paper. Put down the major points you want to make, without regard to their order or relationship. Attach reminders about data, anecdotes, and examples you'll want to use. Circle the main ideas and number them in the order you want them to appear.

If you need more information, you'll discover that now (rather than halfway through the project).

When you're ready to go, you'll know exactly where you're going.

Now engage in a little flash typing. Just let the words fly, without worrying about punctuation, spelling, or sentence structure. The key is to capture the essence of each idea and the flow between ideas.

You'll need to go back and edit, of course, but the time it takes to flash-type a rough (very rough) draft and then edit it will be less—possibly much less—than you would have taken pushing your way along, word by tortured word, trying to create perfection as you go.

On the off chance you don't know how to type fluently, or if you have trouble composing on the keyboard, and if your work life entails significant amounts of writing, you will save yourself incredible amounts of time and frustration by taking the time to learn touch typing and to accustom yourself to composing on the keyboard. It will feel unnatural at first, but you'll soon learn how to think with your fingers.

3. Sustain the Flow

Take breaks before you need them. Writing is one of the most tiring things you can do while sitting down. Don't wait until you're exhausted. Stretch, take a walk, get some water, and return to the battle.

Don't wait until you're stuck to stop, either for a break or at the end of a day's session. If you do, you'll carry a sense of dread around with you. When you sit down to begin again, you'll have a tough time getting started.

Break knowing exactly how you'll continue. Jot yourself a few notes on the next two or three points you want to make. You'll be ready to start without a warm-up.

4. Finish Cleanly

You've said what you needed to say. Now you need to come up with the Big Finish, right?

Wrong.

Trying to come up with an important-sounding conclusion is another waste of time. If the piece of writing is long, reiterate the main idea or recap the main points. If it's short, simply end strongly with your final point.

5. Edit by the Numbers

You've written fast and loose—and the writing shows it. You've got some editing to do.

If possible, arrange your work schedule so that you can set the still-steaming writing aside and do something else before you try to revise. That usually means getting the rough draft done far enough ahead of deadline, and that's a matter of good planning.

The cooling-off period will allow you to gain some objectivity (although you will never be totally objective about your own work, and you shouldn't be).

Don't micro edit until you've macro cut. Go through with an ax, chopping out the repetitious, the irrelevant, and the rambling.

Now go over whatever remains, using a checklist of the specific problems you need to look for, misspellings and dangling modifiers, maybe, and also the almost-right word, the soft passive voice construction, the vague reference.

Where will you get such a checklist? You'll create one by keeping a pad of paper with you as you edit the next couple of pieces you've written, noting the sorts of mistakes you tend to make.

That's another one of those tasks that take a little bit of time now but save tons of time from now on.

If you want a reference to help you with the editing, keep the *Associated Press Style Book* handy to settle questions such as 6:00 a.m., 6:00 A.M., or 6:00 am, for example. For grammar and structure questions, you can rely on *The Elements of Style*, by Will Strunk and E. B. White.

A CAUTIONARY NOTE ABOUT EDITING

Don't even think about not doing it.

You'll save a little time, all right. But you'll spend that time and more, writing the second and third memo clarifying the first one, holding the meeting to explain what you really meant, or explaining to the boss why your report caused the client to cancel the contract.

No amount of time or effort will salvage your damaged reputation.

THE PROS AND CONS OF INSTANT WRITING

We've come a long way from letters chiseled on stone tablets or scrawled with sticks in the dirt.

Electronic mail offers a number of time-saving advantages:

- You eliminate the time it takes to print and deliver a message. Written communication can become almost instant, like a telephone call.
- E-mail is interactive. I ask. You answer. I ask again. You clarify. I propose. You modify.
- Just as the sender can choose when to initiate a message, the receiver can choose when and if to read and respond to it.
- E-mail messages can go to dozens or even hundreds of people at the same time.

E-mail also carries liabilities:

- Because you can send it so fast, you might send it too fast (and wish you hadn't).
- The receiver may not respond in a timely manner.

With call waiting and voice mail, the telephone now offers the same opportunities for evasion, of course.

- A "private" e-mail message may not be so private.

But paper has a way of falling into the wrong hands sometimes, too. The problem here is that e-mail creates the illusion of privacy. Don't be fooled. Don't e-mail it if it can hurt you.

- An "erased" e-mail message may remain in somebody's file.

But that's also true of paper. You only thought all of the copies had been destroyed.

- The delivery system doesn't improve the quality of the message.

You still need to think, organize, write, and revise—all while keeping your goals and your audience's needs in mind. We haven't invented the technology to do the creating for us.

Is e-mail worth the risks?

Absolutely, if . . .

You must discipline your use of e-mail or risk getting caught up in a time-gobbling, mind-numbing round of point-counterpoint dialogue. You may need to establish e-mail–free zones in your day.

E-mail is a great tool—and nothing more. Select it when it's the best method of communication in a given situation. There'll still be room for the confidential written memo and for the announcement tacked on the bulletin board.

Chapter 15

Drowning in a Sea of Paper?

Learn How to Control the Flood

Where does the time go?

You're spending from half to 70 percent of your working time dealing with paper—writing it, reading it, filing it, looking through it for another paper.

That's where the time goes.

The coming of the computer was supposed to usher in the Era of the Paperless Office, but if anything, computers have increased the flow of paper.

If you're ever going to get control of your time—which is to say your life—you're going to have to control the paper flood.

What to do? Here are ten suggestions for getting a hold on it.

10 WAYS YOU CAN REDUCE, CONTROL, AND ELIMINATE PAPER

1. Adopt a Constant Companion

Keep a notebook with you all the time—in your attaché case, in your desk drawer, in your coat pocket or purse, on your night table. Capture those stray insights and write yourself reminders. This way you won't lose your ideas, and you won't wind up with scraps of paper cluttering your life.

2. Manage Your Desktop(s)

A place for everything and everything in its place, on the actual desktop and the virtual one in the computer.

We're not talking neatness here. We're talking organization. Your desktop may extend to the floor and every other flat surface not already covered. But as long as you know where everything is and can lay your hands on it without having to wade through the stuff you don't want, you're in good shape.

Be honest with yourself, though. Do you *really* need all that stuff out in the open where you can see—and trip over—it? You may simply be worried that you'll lose it or forget to deal with it if you can't keep an eye on it. But careful organization and an accessible file cabinet will take care of that problem and help you clean up your working space, too.

3. Touch It Once

How many times do you pick up the same piece of paper, glance at it, scowl, and toss it back on the desk, promising yourself that you'll deal with it later?

Want to find out?

Old-time gunslingers were said to cut notches on the handles of their pistols to represent each conquest. You can keep track of the number of times a sheet of paper slays you—not with notches, but with stickers. Simple dots will do. Every time you handle the paper, slap a dot on it. After a week of dotting, gather up the clutter on your desk and count the dots.

Get the picture?

The first time you handle print—from a one-page memo to a 500-page report—you should decide what to do with it. Then you should do it. Your choices are:

- Reroute (pass it on to someone else who should have it)
- Respond (then file it)
- Read (then file it)
- Recycle (as in, throw it in the recycle bin)

4. Exercise Good Sortsmanship

Start by asking a variation on that fundamental question we developed a few chapters back: *Do I want or need to deal with this?*

If not, does *anybody* need to?

If so, reroute.

If not, recycle.

Do it now. Keep a supply of routing slips, interoffice mail envelopes, and whatever else you need to send the stuff on its way right away. And keep a bucket for recycling within easy arm's reach.

For anything that makes it past this first cut, create a simple system for categorizing every piece of paper you encounter. You don't need anything fancy here. File folders will do fine. You may need no more than three files: "do," "read," and "file."

5. Make It Disappear

There's only one thing better than getting rid of it as soon as you touch it, and that's never having to touch it at all.

Never automatically renew a subscription without balancing the periodical's worth to you with the time it takes to process it. Don't be shy about asking to be taken off mailing lists and routing slips.

For a wholesale purge of third-class mail, write to the Direct Marketing Association, Mail Reference Service, Box 3861, New York, New York 10163-3861 and get off all those lists!

6. RSVP ASAP

If the paper needs only a brief response, do it right now. Create a speed response:

- A personalized Post-it note
- A note written on the bottom of the original letter or memo
- A half-sheet of business letterhead for a short note
- A phone call if appropriate and more efficient

Are you being callous by sending the correspondent's own paper back to her? Not at all. Callous is putting off the response or not responding at all. You're being responsive and smart, and you're also saving paper.

7. File It and Forget It?
Do you really need to keep it?

Most of us never read or even touch three quarters of the stuff we file. Why take the time to file it now and to fumble over it dozens or even hundreds of times in the future? Practice source-point pollution control.

If you do need to hang onto it, put it in the filing folder. Schedule a short filing session once a day (or week or month, depending on the volume of paper you're dealing with), for a time when you're not at your mental peak. (See Chapter 20 on biorhythms for more tips on how to match your energy level and alertness to the task you need to perform.)

8. Strip, Clip, and Flip
Tear out the material you really need and toss the rest of the publication away. Be especially attentive to lists, tabulations, charts, and graphs that summarize a great deal of material in a small space. Then recycle the rest.

While you're at it, toss out periodicals more than a year old, earlier drafts of written material, old reports that no longer have relevance. Schedule a brief session at the end of each week so the clutter level never gets unmanageable. While you're engaged in this relatively mindless work, you can decompress from a hard week of work, ease your transition into evening and weekend leisure time, and reflect on lessons learned.

9. Shift Gears When You Read
Reading everything at the same rate and in the same way makes as much sense as driving at the same speed on all roads and under all conditions.

You can skim some materials for main ideas, scan others for specific information, speed-read still others for the essence.

Save the material that requires time and concentration for your peak energy times and for times when you can concentrate without interruption. Reading difficult material requires your best effort, not the last shreds of consciousness at the end of the day.

10. The Cop-Out Compost Heap

If you can adhere to the "touch it once" rule at all times, you'll save yourself tons of time. You'll also qualify for the Time Management Hall of Fame.

If that rule's a little too rigid, create another file category, the compost heap.

Can't decide what to do with it? Not sure you should do anything at all? Put it in the compost file and forget it.

Once a week, get out the pitch fork and turn that compost. Some of the stuff will have gotten a bit ripe; you'll want to deal with that right away. But you'll find that a lot of the stuff is now ready to go directly to the recycle bin—do not pass go, and do not waste your time.

Paper management will soon become a happy habit, one that will save you enormous amounts of time and remove a lot of the frustration from the workday.

Chapter 16

How Long Since You've Seen Your Desk?

Learn How To Cut Through the Clutter

Are you suffering from Stacked Desk Syndrome or, worse, the dread Piled Floor Phenomenon?

Take a look around your workplace. Do you like what you see?

We're not talking about passing a white glove inspection here, or even about looking presentable when company comes. If your workplace doesn't have to do double duty as reception area, the way it looks really only has to suit you.

But the clutter may be causing you to waste precious time picking through paper, searching for that important document, or simply moving piles from one place to another.

Look at it this way: every piece of paper requires you to do something with it, and doing something with paper takes time. The more times you have to shuffle, stack, file, or forge through the same paper, the more that paper costs you in time.

Here's a simple two-question test you can use to determine whether the level of clutter in your workplace constitutes a time management problem for you:

CLUTTER QUESTION #1: CAN YOU FIND IT?

Be honest now. Do you *really* know right where everything is? Can you put your hands on that important document while you're on the phone with an important client? When necessary, can you tell somebody else how to find the file you want them to bring along for you to the big meeting?

If not, clutter is costing you.

CLUTTER QUESTION #2: ARE YOU COMFORTABLE WITH THINGS THE WAY THEY ARE?

Some folks function just fine amidst the chaos of a heaped-up desk and files strewn all over the conference table. But others are nervous in such surroundings and constantly entertain a little voice in their heads whispering "Clean it up, you slob!" when they're trying to concentrate on more important things.

Again, be honest here. Is your work environment getting in your way in more ways than the obvious, physical ones? If so, clutter is slowing you down as surely as if you were carrying the mess around on your back.

After taking a hard look at your work space and giving honest answers to these two clutter questions, if you can honestly say that clutter isn't a problem for you, that you're just fine with and function efficiently with things just the way they are, here's a time-saving tip for you—skip the rest of this chapter. Don't fix it if it isn't broken, right?

But, if clutter is a problem, read on.

If you're going to get control of your time, you're going to have to control the flood of paper in you life.

What to do? Here are two solutions that, unfortunately, only work for a few.

IMPRACTICAL SOLUTION #1: LET SOMEBODY ELSE CULL THE PAPER

Editors deal with more paper than just about anyone else. How do they manage? At large publications, book publishers, and agencies, the top editors have underlings who turn the flood of incoming material into a manageable trickle before it ever reaches the decision maker. Call them associate editors, or editorial assistants, or goalies—whatever you call them, their job is to read through the "slush" of unsolicited material, diverting all but the most promising projects.

Many executives have assistants to open and sort the mail, dealing with anything that doesn't need the boss's attention.

Ronald Reagan trusted his staffers to encapsulate long reports into "mini-memos" of a page or less.

But many of us don't have such assistants. In fact, many of us *are* the assistants, dealing with the paper someone above us on the organizational chart doesn't want to waste time on.

What are these folks to do with all that paper?

IMPRACTICAL SOLUTION #2: TRAIN YOUR SOURCES TO LIMIT THE PAPER

Ecologists now tell us that it's usually easier and more effective to limit the pollution at its source than to try to clean it up later.

Many paper managers have learned the same lesson.

Editors won't look at an entire manuscript. They demand instead a query letter, a page or less outlining the project and asking if the editor wants to see more.

Perhaps you can train your correspondents to keep it to a page, too.

Then again, perhaps not.

Most of us are going to have to solve the paper problem ourselves. But that's only right, since we usually create the problem for ourselves, too.

WHY DO WE MAKE THE MESS?

"I just don't have time to keep things straightened up?"

That's always the problem, isn't it? That's the reason you started reading this book in the first place.

But, as you've already seen in so many areas of life, time isn't really the problem. We make time for the things we want or need to do.

So, if you don't think you have time to straighten up, you may simply not be placing a high enough priority on cutting through the chaos. But once you recognize how much time you're actually spending messing with the mess, you'll be ready to move clean-up way up on your priority list.

But there are other, more subtle reasons why we learn to live with our piles instead of restoring order.

1. The Nesting Instinct

All those piles of stuff may actually be offering you some comfort or reassurance, a homey "lived in" look, a sense that you belong in this place and the place belongs to you. By your messes you may be marking your territory. (Let's not push the analogy too far, you say?)

If that's the case, removing the clutter will cause discomfort, at least at first. You may feel somewhat lost in an environment that suddenly seems bare and unfriendly.

But you can be neat without being monastic. You can keep those talismans, pictures of loved ones, the autographed poster of Jerry Garcia you've treasured since the 1960s, whatever. You just need to make sure that you can get your work done efficiently and that you can find the things you need when you need them.

2. Saver Spillover

"You just never know when you might need it."

Is that you, justifying saving that restaurant receipt from the business trip you took to Sheboygan six years ago or the copy of the annual facilities maintenance report or the schedule from last year's conference or . . .?

If you're an indiscriminate saver, the clutter is a natural although unintended by-product. You don't really want the clutter, but you'll put up with it as the price you have to pay to hold onto every scrap of paper that has ever crossed your desk.

Ah, but by now you probably *do* know if you're really going to need that paper again. If you're not sure, think about a similar document, something you've been hanging onto for a year or more. In all that time, have you ever needed it?

3. Out of Sight, Out of Mind

Deep down, you may be afraid that, if you can't see it, you'll lose it. Or perhaps your secret dread is that if you don't keep the project out on your desk, you'll forget to finish it. You're using the clutter as a visual cue.

But all those "cues" are getting in each other's way and yours. That folder you really need is covered up, out of sight, lost if not forgotten.

4. The Einstein Complex

Thomas Edison had a messy lab. Albert Einstein didn't even wear socks, much less a matching pair.

Clutter is a sign of creativity, right?

You may on some level believe that your clutter marks you as an inventive and busy person. And besides, you like the notoriety your mess has earned for you and the good-natured teasing folks give you about it.

Bad news, folks. There just isn't a whole lot of evidence to support the notion that creativity correlates positively with a messy desk, and truth to tell, sloppy isn't really all that cute.

It's just messy.

And the mess is costing you time.

If you're ready, then, it's time to cut the clutter. Take the time now, and you'll save the time every hour you're in your newly organized environment.

SMALL STEPS, BIG STRIDES

Nobody simply—in one sitting—writes a novel, creates a five-year plan, or blasts the faces of four former presidents out of the stern stone of Mt. Rushmore. We do big projects in small increments, one manageable segment at a time.

Same goes for conquering the clutter.

It took you a long time to accumulate all that. Short of dousing the stuff with kerosene, tossing a lighted match on it, and running, there's no quick way to divest yourself of it, either.

You're going to do it five minutes at a time.

Pledge that, for as long as the job takes, you're going to devote five minutes of every work hour to clutter removal. For every hour you're working but not otherwise obligated to attend a meeting or give a presentation, take the final five minutes to attack the mess.

Start with those piles on the desk. Pick up six or seven inches worth and go through, paper by paper, file by file, periodical by periodical.

If you need to do something about, with, or to it, don't do it now! But do determine what you will do and when, and make a note to yourself to do it. Only then are you safe in putting it in the "to do" basket.

If you need to keep it, grab a file folder and a marking pen. Create categories that work for you, key words that will enable you to find the material easily later. Make the categories general enough to help you consolidate dozens of singles into just a few composites. A file folder marked "Minutes of the June 3, 1997 board meeting" will only serve you once and is only marginally better than the loose minutes themselves. But a file folder marked "Board minutes, 1997" creates a neat receptacle for 12 sets of papers.

Ah, but do you really need to save those board minutes at all?

Keep the recycle basket close at hand, too. If you don't really need it, never use it, can just as easily get the copy on file in the administrative assistant's office, already have a summary that's just as good and much more convenient—get rid of it.

When the five minutes are up, go back to your regular tasks, setting a timer if necessary to remind you to take the next anti-clutter break in 55 minutes.

You may find yourself refreshed and better able to get back to work, feeling psychologically pounds lighter as the pounds of paper diminish.

When the desk is under control, go after those file cabinets. Toss out entire folders of material that are no longer relevant. Go through the keeper files page by page, culling the stuff you don't need.

Hey, you didn't really need a new file cabinet after all. After a few cleaning sessions, there's plenty of room in the old one! And everything in there is a lot easier to find.

These five-minute clear-out drills may soon become a happy habit, a cleansing break you actually look forward to. You'll gain momentum for the task as you see the mess begin to melt away and an efficient work space emerge.

ONGOING MAINTENANCE

Sadly, a large majority of the people who lose weight on diets gain all the weight back—often with interest.

While on that diet, you may totally change your eating habits. But if you go back to old behavior patterns when you attain your target weight, the weight inevitably sneaks back.

Same with work space clutter. Shedding the unwanted pounds of paper is one thing; keeping them off is quite another.

You'll still need to devote a set amount of time each working day to clutter control, perhaps not five minutes an hour anymore, maybe more like 15 minutes at the end of the day, whatever it takes to make sure the mess doesn't creep back in.

You'll also need to apply good paper management techniques to the incoming paper flow.

INCOMING!

Schedule a time each workday to deal with the incoming mail and memos. Be prepared with waste and recycle baskets, calendar, address book, file folders, Post-its, and stick-em dots. Now you're ready for a six-step process to reduce, control, and eliminate paper.

1. Toss envelopes immediately. If you need to save an address, note it in your address book or write it on a Post-it note and stick it to the letter or report.

2. Note meeting and other appointment times on your calendar. And then, unless you need the paper for some other reason, get rid of it.

3. Create the file now. If you need to save a document (are you *sure*?) and don't already have a place for it (are you sure of *that*, too?), create the file for it now, mark it carefully, and put it away.

And you get to move on to the next task with clear conscience and clear desk.

4. Schedule it. If the material is going to require a longer and more thoughtful response, jot yourself a quick note on a Post-it indicating what you want to say and do and stick the note to the page. Don't toss it on the "to-do later" pile until you've also noted on your schedule exactly when you'll deal with it.

5. Prune the periodicals. You may be on the routing list for a lot of periodicals you don't really need to read. But even handling that newsletter, deciding not to read it, and sending it along to the next name on the list require time. Get yourself off those routing lists.

Skim those periodicals you do need to attend to. If you find something you want to read, clip it from the periodical if it's yours, or make a photocopy if it isn't. Then get rid of the unwanted remainder. Put your clips and copies in a "current reading" folder for that scheduled reading time or for the next time you're stuck waiting in an airport or reception area.

6. Affix the deadly red dot. It doesn't have to be a red dot. Any color will do. But whatever color you pick, stick a dot (or star or happy face) on pieces of paper you aren't going to file, toss, recycle, or turn around during your current session.

Keep those dots handy. The next time you handle that piece of paper, stick another dot on it. Do this every time you have to pick up the paper, even if just to move it out of the way to get at something else.

You'll get mighty sick of sticking those dots. And you'll create a vivid visual testimony to the amount of time managing every stray sheet of paper requires of you.

This will lead you to apply steps one through six ever more rigorously.

It will also prompt you to question yourself every time you feel the impulse to make a photocopy, print out e-mail, or clip an article. If you make it, you'll have to manage it.

Keeping in shape is a lot easier than getting back in shape. Deflect the incoming and manage the day-to-day, so that clutter never again becomes a time-consuming problem. Good paper management will save you enormous amounts of time and spare you needless frustration every working day.

Chapter 17

Tired of Waiting?

Learn How to Turn Downtime into Your Most Productive Time

When you were a kid, I'll bet you spent a lot of time waiting and wishing. I know I did.

Mondays, I'd start waiting and wishing for Fridays.

About the time I got to school each day, I'd start waiting and wishing for recess, and then lunch, and then the magic hour of 3:00, time to go home. I can't imagine how much time I spent staring at time, in the form of those clunky old school clocks, the kind that went "click-thunk" each time the big hand struggled another minute forward. (Was it my imagination, or did the "click-thunks" get louder for the final two or three minutes of each hour?)

The more I looked, the slower that minute hand moved. So I'd play the waiting game, trying to make myself wait 15 minutes between clock checks. I rarely made it that long.

Along about Halloween, I started waiting and wishing for Christmas. After Christmas, there was still New Year's Day, a wonderful occasion for a kid who got to go to the Tournament of Roses Parade almost every year. But January 2nd I started waiting and wishing for baseball season, and once baseball season finally arrived, the wait for summer vacation became all but intolerable.

After a few weeks of the endless, unstructured days of summer, I sometimes caught myself—No! Not wishing for school! Never that! But feeling twinges of something that just might have been boredom. So I'd start wishing and waiting for our family's annual two-week trek to some mountain lake. After that I could look forward to my late-summer birthday.

Then the cycle of waiting and wishing started all over again. You, too?

WHY DON'T ADULTS GET BORED?

It seemed like such a problem when you were a kid.

"Mom, I'm bored," you'd whine, drawing "bored" out to seven syllables.

Mom would suggest a list of a dozen or so of your favorite activities, but you were tired of them all. She then might suggest that you kill a little time by working it to death mowing the lawn or cleaning your room or . . . .

Ah. Boredom isn't a lack of things to do, after all. It's a lack of anything you *want* to do. Boredom is equal parts restlessness (exhausted people don't get bored; they fall asleep) and "lack-of-want-to," complete disinterest in or aversion to any of the possible activities you might do next.

So, how come we never seem to get bored now?

We still get restless, although less frequently and intensely as we mature (read "become more frequently exhausted"). And we certainly continue to suffer from lackawanna (more or less frequently and intensely in inverse proportion to how much we genuinely enjoy our work and family life). But always we suffer, too, from too much to do and too little time to do it. We push on to the next task, damn the lackawanna, full speed ahead.

Also, as we get older, we become aware of the dwindling number of days left to us. Even the Mondays in February become more precious in that context, and we become loath to wish any of our time away.

What would you give for one of those endless Christmas Eve days of your youth, when time seemed to crawl and the hours refused to pass?

Fact is, you still have them, probably several little Christmas Eve days each working day. It's called waiting.

We wait for the coffee to perk, wait for the bus to come, wait for somebody to unjam the copy machine, wait for the client to respond to our voice mail message, wait for our luncheon date, wait in traffic, wait at the doctor's office or the Quicky Lube (which can never be quite Quicky enough). Time passes slowly at these times, not because we're anticipating the joy of good surprises under the Christmas tree, but because we need to be elsewhere, doing other things.

Most of us hate waiting. The more crowded your to-do list or day planner and the more impatient you tend to be, the more excruciating the waiting. We've reacted by trying to speed up our activity and eliminate the spaces between activities so we can cram more of them into a day.

ONE BAD WAY TO DO AWAY WITH WAITING

Folks who are always late never have to wait. They make everybody else wait. That's one solution to the problem of waiting.

In the world of academia, the amount of time students are allegedly required to wait for their teachers is a function of the teacher's position on the status pole. Teaching assistants and lecturers get little or no leeway. The untenured assistant prof gets less slack than his tenured associate professor colleague, and a student walks out of a tardy full professor's class at his or her peril unless at least 15 minutes have elapsed.

This scale is well known to many professors but virtually unknown to most students (who probably don't know their teacher's rank anyway).

But in most areas of life, relative status and power often dictate how long folks will wait for one another. The other determinant, of course, is dependency. You may not afford your plumber many status points, but you'll wait for him or her indefinitely as you keep swapping an empty bucket for a full one under the oozing water pipe.

How long are people required to wait for you? How long are they willing? What will they think of you while they wait?

I suspect that keeping people waiting isn't really your style anyway. Folks who seek help with time management are generally the ones being kept late by others. You get places on time, and you expect others to do the same.

That's one reason why for you waiting is inevitable.

I've suggested that you build time cushions into your daily life. But when you allow more travel time than you might need under perfect circumstances and, by some miracle, circumstances actually turn out to be perfect, you'll show up places early. That means even more waiting.

ONE OKAY WAY TO ELIMINATE SOME OF THE WAITING

Folks who keep you waiting tend to do so chronically. You can eliminate some of the waiting in your life by eliminating some of those people.

Stand me up once, shame on you. Stand me up twice, shame on me. I don't make a second appointment with the person who blew off the first one.

But we don't always have a choice. One of the chronic wait-creators in your life might be your boss, your spouse, or your kid. You can try to convert these folks into the cult of punctuality, but you'll most likely fail.

That's another reason why you'll have to wait sometimes.

YOU MIGHT BE ABLE TO MAKE THE WAIT MATTER LESS

You know certain activities will involve waiting. To the extent that it's in your power to do so, try to engage in those activities at times when waiting won't make as big a difference.

But few doctors schedule appointments for 6:00 (a.m. or p.m.) or Saturday afternoons. You have to take what you can get, including the cancellation at the dentist right in the middle of the day, just one more reason why . . .

YOU'LL *ALWAYS* HAVE TO WAIT

Three inescapable facts of modern life make waiting unavoidable.

- There's too many of us in the same place.
- We're all trying to get someplace else.
- We get in each other's way doing it.

No matter which line you pick at the market or the bank, the line you pick will move the slowest, right? (When my wife and I run errands together, we hedge our bets by standing in separate lines. We even make a friendly competition out of it to see whose line "wins.") You'll always wind up behind the person with 26 items in the "12 Items or Less" line. That person will wait until those 26 items have been scanned and totaled before beginning to think about paying. And then the miscreant will drag out a change purse and pay in pennies, 4,284 of them.

What can you do? You can rant and bellow. You can make snide comments under your breath. You can dump your groceries on the ground and walk away. You can switch to another line—and wind up behind someone who wants to get a refund on a quart of ice cream purchased at another store, in another decade.

Or you can take what seems to be a lemon and make lemonade.

HOW TO USE THE WAIT TIME: THREE STEPS THAT WILL MAKE YOU MORE PRODUCTIVE *AND* LESS RUSHED

Step 1. Accept the Wait as Inevitable

Waiting is destructive for two reasons. First, if you haven't allowed sufficient time for waiting, the wait will destroy your schedule and cause you to be late for other appointments and to fail to complete necessary tasks. You can defuse this time bomb, lowering the stakes in the waiting game, by refusing to overpack the schedule. That way, the wait can't hurt you as much.

But waiting can be even more destructive because of what it does to your insides. Oh, how we seethe as we idle in traffic or jiggle and fidget in the waiting room. That seething can trigger a corrosive stress reaction, harming us physically as well as emotionally.

You may not be able to eliminate the wait, but you can minimize the damage it can do to you by accepting what you can't change. Stop blaming the fates (or the jerk who kept you waiting). Stop festering about where you should be and what you should be doing. Be where you are, doing what you're doing.

Step 2. Rename the Wait

You speed through the day, pushing your body and mind beyond fatigue, putting off needed rest...

- *until* you get home and can finally kick off your shoes and put your feet up, or
- *until* the kids are fed and bathed and storied and put to bed, or
- *until* the weekend, or
- *until* the vacation, or
- *until* retirement, or . . .

Some of those untils never come, of course. And sometimes when they do, they come too late to help, because you've already been pushed past the point where you *can* relax.

Meanwhile, you may have rushed and squirmed and fretted your way through four or five potential rest periods a day.

Rename the wait. Call it a rest instead.

Oh, what a difference. Waits are cold frustrations. Rests are warm comforts.

Could you really feel warm and embraced stuck in the middle of traffic? Probably not right away. Such a major change in mind-set takes some working at and some getting used to. But it can be done. I know it, because I've done it—not right away, and not every time, but often enough that I now realize the anger and frustration aren't inevitable results of waiting.

Step 3. Use the Wait

You're running late, racing the green turn arrow to the intersection. But the bozo in front of you is poking along, blissfully unaware of your need to make that signal. The bozo, of course, makes the light while causing you to miss it. It's just one of the unwritten laws of physics.

You can scream and fume, spiking your blood pressure while adrenaline oozes out your ears. Or you can proclaim a rest and take one of your mini-vacations for deep breathing or mental roaming.

Too unproductive for you? Spend 45 seconds visualizing a perfect golf swing or tennis stroke. (There's evidence that positive visualization might even improve your stroke or swing.)

Conduct a mental dialogue with someone you've always wanted to talk to.

Brainstorm solutions to a problem.

Plan a week's worth of dinner menus.

You'll wait a lot longer than 45 seconds at the doctor's office. So come prepared. Bring that book you've been trying to find time to read, or the crossword puzzle you'll never have time for later.

Tend to your knitting.

Write a haiku.

Read one of those moldy magazines that seem to survive only in historical societies and waiting rooms (okay, and my basement). Pick something you wouldn't usually read. For me that might be *Cosmopolitan*, *Modern Maturity*, or *Highlights for Children*. I tend to catch up on *People* that way, too. You'll gain a new perspective on life and learn things you never would have known. And that way it won't make any difference that the magazine is old; it's all new to you anyway.

RESULTS OF TURNING THE WAIT INTO A REST

You'll be better rested and more relaxed (and better read).

You'll be more efficient and effective.

Who knows? You might write some great haiku.

And you'll get to where you were going at exactly the same time you would have anyway.

Chapter 18

Are You Paying a High Price for Procrastination?

Learn How to Put Off the Urge to Put It Off

The national association of procrastinators met recently in Houston, Texas, for their annual gathering. I wonder how many of them were late?

I was going to check, but I never got around to it.

Like all our other human failings, procrastination makes great subject matter for jokes. But real-life procrastination is no laughing matter.

No time management technique will do you a whit of good if you still allow yourself to postpone the difficult or the unpleasant. The job doesn't get any less unpleasant while you wait. Quite the contrary, your sense of dread will build, making it increasingly difficult to bring yourself to the task.

And it won't get any easier, either. Rather, your delay will merely complicate matters. You'll have to deal with the complications, often before you can even get at the original job.

Thus, procrastination costs time while creating unnecessary stress.

So, if it's so awful, how come so many of us do it? Why are there some jobs we just never seem to "get around to," no matter the consequences of our evasion?

FIVE REASONS WHY WE PROCRASTINATE AND FIVE STRATEGIES TO PUT OFF PUTTING OFF

Reason 1. You Haven't Really Committed to Doing the Job

When I teach a workshop for would-be and beginning novelists, I often start by asking why they want to write a novel. Such an extended project demands a huge commitment of time, energy, and emotion, after all. Most of the answers I get fall into one of three categories.

The first reason, simply stated, is that the writer feels good while writing (or, conversely, feels wretched when denied the opportunity to write). For some, writing seems to be almost an addiction or a compulsion, although a relatively harmless one.

The second set of reasons basically cluster around the notion of communication and storytelling: "I have something to say, and a novel seems to be the best way to say it," or "I've got a story I want or need to tell." I've even heard folks say that the story seems to be using them to get itself told.

The third set of reasons stems from the notion, sadly mistaken, that novelists become rich and famous with relatively little effort. Many of the folks in this group don't want to write a novel; they want to have written a novel, so they can reap the supposed rewards.

Most of the folks in the first category and many in the second actually go on to write that novel. Few in the third group ever do.

Occasionally I get a reason that doesn't fall into any of these categories.

"My English teacher back in good old P.S. 134 said I'd make a good novelist," one might say, or "Folks in my book group think my life story would be inspirational."

Assuming that they aren't being coy, that they don't really mean "I think I'd make a great novelist," or "I think my life story would be inspirational," my response to this sort of reason borders on Mom's old admonition: "If somebody told you to jump off a cliff, would you do it?"

The key here is the source of the motivation. We generally don't need to *prioritize* or otherwise force or trick ourselves into performing actions that are internally motivated. But the more the motivation comes from the English teacher or the book club or the mate or the boss or any other external source, the less likely we are to do it.

Know anybody who got into the family bakery business, or became a lawyer, or joined the Marines because somebody expected or demanded it? If so, you probably know an unhappy baker or lawyer or Marine.

You may chronically put off an activity because you aren't really sold on doing it at all. Reasons include:

- You don't think it's your job.
- You think it's somebody else's job.
- The job's a waste of time.

If that's the case, you need to answer two fundamental questions:

- What's in it for me if I do it?
- What will happen to me if I don't?

The first question may redirect and increase your motivation. You're no longer doing it because someone said you ought to. You're doing it to impress a boss, help a friend, make money, or get to a task you really enjoy.

The second question is the negative of the first. Your motivation may become avoidance of something unpleasant, like a lousy job evaluation, an angry, alienated spouse, or a disappointed child, for example.

If you can find no internal motivation—no benefit for doing the job and no penalty for not doing it, you may well decide not to do it at all.

Even if you can see a benefit to doing the job, you may still decide that the costs in time and energy (and the other things you aren't doing) outweigh the benefits. In that case you can

1. Do what you have to do to get out of the job. That's not the same thing as simply putting it off. This is a definitive decision not to do it and to accept the consequences, if any. In the long run, that sort of decision costs less, in time and stress, than does the passive resistance of procrastination.

Or

2. Do it anyway—but for your own reasons.

Reason 2. You're Afraid of the Job

This is a hard thing for many of us to admit—to ourselves let alone to someone else. But it may be what's keeping you from doing a job you need and want to accomplish. If you can identify your reluctance as fear and track it to its source, you can deal with the fear and get on with the job. Here are three of the most common varieties of performance anxiety:

- Fear of failure

Consider the student who never studies and flunks out. He can always tell himself, "If I had studied, I would have passed the stupid course." But what if he had studied—and still failed?

For most of us, "won't" is a lot easier to deal with than "can't." If you don't try it, you don't have to confront the possibility that you can't do it.

- Fear of success

On the other hand, if you do pass the course, folks will expect you to do it again, or to go out and get a job, or to apply what you've learned. If you never try, you'll never have to face the consequences of success, either.

- Fear of finishing

"If I pass the course, I'll graduate. If I graduate, I'll . . ."
You'll what?
If you don't pass the course, you'll never have to find out what happens next.
If you never write the novel, you'll never have to know whether a publisher would have accepted it.
If you don't finish basic training, you'll never have to know whether you could have really hacked it in the military.
Sometimes the not knowing seems more acceptable than the possible consequences of finding out for sure.
But how sad to let such fears prevent you from ever trying.
Identify the fear. Give it a name and confront it. Imagine the consequences of your actions or non-actions as objectively as you can.
The fear won't go away. But if the goal is worth pursuing, you'll be able to act despite the fear.

Reason 3. You Don't Place a High Enough Priority on the Activity
You're sold on the idea that somebody ought to do the task. You'll even agree, if pressed, that you're the person to do it. You may even want to do it.
You just don't want or need to do it enough, and you always want or need to do something else more.
Thus, the poor task—cleaning the leaves out of the rain gutters in autumn, to cite one mundane example—keeps getting bumped down the list, below other, more pressing jobs. You've got to go grocery shopping first, because you won't have anything to eat if you don't. You've got to mow the lawn first, because it will look awful if you don't. (And nobody can see the leaves in the rain gutters, after all.)

This sort of procrastination problem may eventually work itself out. As the other tasks get done, those leafy gutters work their way up the list. Or the problem may take on a higher priority after the first hard rain of the season.

Establishing priorities is subjective, especially when dealing with activities that are neither urgent nor particularly important relative to other activities. Take a look at the job that just isn't getting done and see if you can redefine it in terms of the ultimate benefit you'll receive for doing it.

First time through, this definition may be negative:

"If I don't clean out the rain gutters, I'll get a flood in the garden the first time it rains hard."

Positive motivations tend to be much stronger. Recast it in the positive form:

"If I clean out the rain gutters, I'll protect my garden from flooding."

Is that important to you?

Are there other ancillary benefits to getting the task done?

- "I'll finally stop worrying about it."
- "I'll get some nice exercise out in the sunshine."
- "I can listen to a ball game on the radio while I work."

Are these considerations enough to move the task up the list? If so, get at it! But if not, you must either resign yourself to living with the consequences of your non-action or find a way to get the job done without actually having to do it. You could hire the neighbor kid, thus trading money for time, for example. Or, you could add "It won't cost anything if I do it myself" to your list of ancillary benefits, perhaps tipping the balance in favor of doing it.

Reason 4. You Don't Know Enough to Do the Task

When I get "writer's block," it's often my subconscious mind's helpful way of suggesting that I don't really know what the hell I'm talking about.

This is true for other sorts of motivational blocks as well. You may simply not know enough to do the job right. You haven't consciously recognized or admitted this to yourself, but you know it deep down, and this knowledge is manifesting itself in strong aversion.

Gather the information you need. If all else fails, read the directions (a desperate last resort for many of us). Then plunge into the task.

Learn to discern between the legitimate need to gather information and a stalling mechanism whereby reading the book or going to talk to the guy at the hardware store is simply a way to put off confronting the job. If your problem is "lack of want to" rather than lack of information, you'll need a different strategy, namely, what to do when...

Reason 5. You Just Plain Don't Wanna!

On a preference scale of 1 to 10, giving Rover his flea bath rates a minus 2.

It isn't merely unpleasant. It isn't just disgusting. It's downright dangerous. Rover does not like his flea bath. Last time you tried this little experiment in torture, you wound up scratched, Rover was traumatized, and the bathroom looked like a tidal wave had hit it.

The fleas are back. Rover is scratching. If you don't do something—and fast—you'll have fleas all over the house.

You've got two choices, and you don't need a book on time management to tell you what they are:

- Gut it out, or
- Farm it out.

Get on the old raincoat, put a tarp down around the tub, and pop Rover into the suds. Or make an appointment with your friendly neighborhood dog groomer.

Identify the reason for the procrastination. Confront your attitudes and fears. Weigh the consequences.

Then deal with it!

Chapter 19

Just Don't Do It!

Learn How to Get Rid of the Tasks
You Don't Want or Need to Do

Much of time management seeks to help us do things faster and do more than one thing at once, so we can fit more doing into the same limited amount of time.

But no time management plan can work without attention to the tasks themselves.

Here's where the famous admonition to "work smarter, not harder" comes into play.

Spend just a little time today questioning some of the tasks you do every day, and you can save tons of time every day from now on.

HOW TO ELIMINATE UNNECESSARY STEPS

"I'm so busy doing the dance," a worker laments, "I haven't got time to learn the steps."

Let's free up some time by eliminating some of those steps, the ones that aren't getting you anywhere.

Get Rid of the Cobweb Catacombs

When I first came to work with the University of Wisconsin Extension, I discovered that every adult education program we offered generated an enormous amount of paperwork, starting with the financial planning form, by which we set the fee for the program, and the instructional form, which gave each program its tracking number. Then came the forms to order mailing labels and brochure duplicating from state printing. The process built through a series of confirmation forms that would have done a NASA countdown proud: six-month confirmation, two-month confirmation, six-week confirmation, two-week confirmation—I began looking for the four-minute confirmation—along with the audiovisual request form, the food and beverage break form, the . . .Well, you get the idea.

It soon became clear to me that some of these forms served no useful purpose to me or to the people planning and teaching the programs with me. This occurred to me because I'm the one who had to pay attention to all those forms (which were, of course, "urgent" and needed "immediate attention").

It took me a little longer to determine that some of the forms didn't do anybody any good at the conference center or the finance office or the printer, either.

We were just doing the forms because we had always done the forms.

And we had always done them in triplicate.

For some reason nobody could explain to me, we needed not just one, not two, but three copies of each form. One went in my files. One went in the department administrator's files. And one went into a file I took to calling the cobweb catacombs.

I decided that, if the department administrator had one in her files, and her files were always open to me, and her office was a mere few steps down the hall from mine, then—Eureka!—I didn't really need to have a copy in my files.

And nobody seemed to need the copy in the cobweb catacombs.

So couldn't we maybe just make one copy?

Those of you enmeshed in the web of a bureaucracy, any bureaucracy, know that it's never that simple. Some folks get extremely threatened by the notion that we might not need to have all that nice paper backing us up.

I did succeed in getting rid of a couple of the forms. And I did eliminate the cobweb catacombs—one small victory in the war on wasted time.

Are a couple of unnecessary forms and an extra step in filing really worth the fight it takes to get rid of them? Depends on how many people you have to fight and how hard you have to fight them. But you *do* have the power to stem some of your daily work flood. You don't need status or tenure if you have common sense and the voice of reason on your side. Couch your proposal in terms of the good of the organization, to achieve the goals you and your boss share, and you have a chance to succeed.

It *is* worth it. It's worth questioning the need for any process that requires your time and attention. Get rid of it now and you draw the benefits every day from now on.

TWO MORE FORMS OF UNNECESSARY WORK—BUSY WORK AND WORK AVOIDANCE WORK

When I worked in construction during summers to put myself through college, I soon discovered that the hardest days I ever put in were the days when there was no work. I had to look busy or catch hell from the superintendent. That meant inventing tasks that made me look like I was doing something constructive without getting in the way of anybody who had real work to do.

I swept a lot of sidewalks, pushing the dirt up to one end of the walk, then turning around and pushing it back down to the other. The supe didn't have to try to invent something for me to do, and I was within shouting range when he did have a job for me. (The man had a *huge* shouting range, believe me!)

I've been in a lot of office settings where bosses created busy work for subordinates rather than have to face the prospect of figuring out something real for them to do (or to endure watching them play computer solitaire).

But I've also caught myself creating busy work for myself because it makes me feel productive. (Those old construction laboring habits die hard.) Also, doing something simple but unnecessary may be a lot easier than actually planning what I ought to be doing next.

When you take a hard look at the things you do, don't just look to eliminate tasks that others ask or require you to do. Get rid of the self-generated busy work, too.

I've also caught myself doing low-priority or unnecessary jobs to avoid doing the harder task I really need to be doing. For me, almost anything is easier than organizing a long, complex piece of writing or engaging in budget planning. It's amazing what I'll do to avoid these. And as long as I'm doing something, I'm just "too busy" to get to the onerous stuff.

In many offices today, the most pervasive form of work avoidance work is "surfing" the net. Web casting certainly keeps you busy, you're undoubtedly learning something (although its application to the workplace may be tenuous), and once you learn to find your way around you start having a wonderful time.

But that seductive screen gobbles time in huge gulps. And while you're "busy" surfing, other work is waiting—work that may put you under severe time pressure later.

Not all net surfing is work avoidance, of course (just as not all sidewalk sweeping is done merely in the cause of looking busy). But the surfer knows how to determine the usefulness of the ride.

When you catch yourself doing work avoidance work, redirect your time and energy.

THE "*NOT*-TO-DO" LIST AND THE "LET-OTHERS-DO-IT" LIST

We do a lot of what we do today because we did it yesterday, and the day before. We're accustomed to doing it, perhaps even in the habit of doing it, and doing it is actually easier than not doing it.

You may need to create a "*not*-to-do" list to remind you of the tasks you've decided to eliminate from your routine. This may seem silly, but that doesn't necessarily mean it's a bad idea. See if the list helps you; just don't let anybody else see it.

Which leads us to those tasks that should be done—but not by *you.*

Make a list of those tasks you now perform but which you feel should be done by someone else. Reasons for putting tasks on this list include:

- I lack the authority to do it right.
- I lack the skill, information, or tools to do it right.
- If I do it, other tasks with higher priorities don't get done.

This list does not, unfortunately, include:

- "I don't want to,"
- "I don't like to," or even
- "It's not in my job description" (although this point probably should become the subject of a future planning discussion with your supervisor).

DELEGATING, SWAPPING, AND LETTING GO

Once you determine that someone else should be doing a job you're now performing, you have three options for getting someone else to do it.

1. Delegating

A lot of folks are fortunate enough to have someone else to answer the phone for them, thus absorbing the interruptions and, of course, screening callers. Some folks have other folks to open and sort their mail for them, too, and make the coffee, and fill out all those stupid forms and a lot of other less-than-glamorous tasks.

Time management books always suggest that we save time by delegating such jobs to others. (Note that this doesn't actually "save" any time. It simply shifts the time from one person to another.)

Unfortunately, this option is open only to bosses. If you have no one to boss, you have to answer your own phone and open your own mail. This time management book is for you, too, so let's explore two other options.

2. Swapping

One program assistant loves to file and fill out forms but dreads answering the telephone. (I believe that phonephobia is much more prevalent in the workplace than any of us would like to admit.)

Another program assistant, working in the same office, hates the paperwork but loves answering the phone.

Not surprisingly, the first assistant doesn't do a very good job with callers, while the second is invariably courteous, cheerful, and helpful.

Neither assistant has the authority to delegate work to the other. But they might be able to arrange a trade, with their supervisor's approval, of course.

3. Letting Go

Some folks don't let anyone else open their mail or answer their telephone because they won't, rather than because they can't.

This may stem from a lack of trust in the subordinate, of course—a bad situation for a variety of reasons, but the inability to let go may not have anything to do with anybody else. Some folks just have a terrible time delegating. Even if they do assign a task to someone else, they find themselves "supervising" so much, they wind up spending as much or more time on it—and alienating the coworker in the process.

When you hand a job off to someone else, don't tie a string to it. Make sure your coworkers know what they're supposed to accomplish, and then *let them accomplish it their way*. If they don't get the desired results in the allotted time, work on these specific outcomes. But keep your hands off the work in progress.

That way you really save the time, and your coworker doesn't have to put up with your fussing.

DO IT NOW, DO IT LATER, OR DO IT NEVER

Does it need a meeting, or will a memo do? Does it need a memo, or will a phone call do? Does it need a phone call? Does it need doing at all?

"Because we've always done it" is a rotten reason to do anything.

Keep those Post-it notes handy. As you plan and direct your work flow, get used to the idea of using three rather than merely two categories: "Do it now," "Do it later," and "Do it never."

Deciding to "do it never" isn't at all the same as simply not doing it. If you toss it back on the pile and push it to the back of your mind, it will continue to clutter your physical and mental space, and it will need dealing with all over again. Make the decision not to do it—and tell anybody whose work is affected by your decision.

If it won't take long, and it doesn't interrupt something important, do it now. If it doesn't carry a high degree of urgency or if you have a task with a higher level of urgency needing your attention, do it later.

Don't let the medium of communication affect your decision. My e-mail announces its arrival with beeps and pulsating icons. The paper mail just sits on the desk. Even if I've turned my e-mail off, I get the beep and the blinking letter in the upper left corner of the screen. But that doesn't make the e-mail message more important than the paper message.

A ringing phone creates a heightened sense of urgency in many of us, but that shouldn't automatically give the caller a higher priority than the person sitting across the table.

If you decide to "do it later," note *when* you'll do it and *what*, specifically, you're going to do. If you don't, your attempts at organizing may degenerate into evasion instead.

PEELING OFF THE LAYERS OF PERFECTION: THE "GOOD ENOUGH" TENET OF TIME MANAGEMENT

You've decided to do it now. Now, how well will you do it? If it has to be perfect before you'll let it go, you've got a big time management problem.

I'm not advocating shoddy work or irresponsible performance. But I suspect that isn't really an issue here. Sloppy, irresponsible people don't read time management books. Conscientious people do. But the line between *conscientious* and *perfectionist* can be hard to find, and perfectionists have a tough time finishing anything.

The computer can make the problem worse. Because we can edit so easily, because we can always surf for more information, because we can run one more set of data at the push of a button, we may raise our quality expectations until we reach such lofty (and utterly ridiculous) pinnacles of perfectionism as "zero tolerance for error." (We might as well ban that horrible time waster, the bathroom break.)

How good is good enough? Who's going to see it? What are they going to do with it?

The meeting minutes that will be filed and forgotten need to be factually accurate and written in clear English; they don't need to be rendered in rhyming couplets.

The agenda for an informal meeting of department heads calls for a lower level of sophistication and polish than does the final draft of the annual report for the stockholders.

Working figures for the preliminary budget meeting don't need to be carried out to 10 places past the decimal point. To the nearest thousand dollars is probably close enough, and more precise calculations are in fact a waste of time, since the numbers will all be changed later.

"Simplify, simplify," Thoreau advised us.

You can't flee to Walden Pond, but you can eliminate unnecessary tasks, delegate or swap others, and give each task an appropriate level of attention.

By managing your tasks, you'll be expanding the amount of time available to you.

Chapter 20

Whose Drum Do You March To?

Learn to Keep Time to Your Own (Bio)rhythms

It's one of life's little ironies: by the time you get old enough to stay up as late as you want to, you're too tired to stay up late.

Just about every kid who ever lived has fought to stay up past bedtime. You, too? If so, the more tired you became, the harder you no doubt fought the inevitable.

"But, Mom," you probably wailed with your last waking breath, "I'm not sleepy!"

You might as well have gone peacefully. You've spent the rest of your life living by the clock rather than by your inclinations.

In the "time before time," people lived by the natural rhythms of the day and the season. They got up when the sun rose, worked and played in the daylight, and went to sleep when the sun went down again.

But ever since Thomas Alva Edison finally found a filament that would get hot enough to glow without burning up, we've been able to defy the cycle of the sun, keeping ourselves awake with artificial light.

We awaken to the clangor of the alarm clock, yanking ourselves out of sleep rather than allowing ourselves to drift naturally up through the layers of sleep into waking. We hurtle out of bed and into the day's obligations, becoming estranged from our own dreams.

We eat by the clock, too, at "meal time," when it fits the schedule, or not at all. We combine work with food, to the detriment of digestion, with the "power breakfast" and the "working lunch" and the "business dinner."

If we become tired at the "wrong" time, like in the middle of the afternoon staff meeting, we fight off fatigue with caffeine or sugar or both, overriding our need for rest.

And we pay for it.

WHAT WOULD YOU DO IF YOU COULD DO WHATEVER YOU WANTED TO?

Most of us have developed a daily cycle involving one long block of from six to nine hours of sleep and two or three meals, the largest coming at dinnertime.

You've trained your body to this cycle (or your own version of it) through repetition and reinforcement, but your body may show its displeasure, by being groggy and sleep-ridden at get-up time, queasy at dinnertime, wakeful at bedtime. You may simply struggle through these discomforts, or you may seek pharmaceutical help to rise, eat, and sleep at the "right" times.

Ever wonder what you'd do if you let yourself do whatever felt right? What if you had absolutely no obligations or appointments, a true vacation? You could get up when you wanted, eat when you wanted, nap if you wanted, stay up all night if you wanted.

You probably wouldn't do much too differently for the first few days. Our learned patterns can become quite entrenched. But after a few days, as you begin at last to relax and ease into a new way of life, what would you ease into?

What if you let the body, rather than the schedule, drive your day?

Scientists have wondered about such things. One experiment involves putting folks into an environment free of all obligations, free of all clocks and watches, even free of sunrise and sunset. Subjects had no schedules to follow and no clues as to when they "should" sleep and wake and eat.

Here's what they taught us by their reactions:

1. **When left to our own devices, we will establish a fairly consistent pattern.**
2. **That pattern varies with the individual.** One schedule does not fit all. What's "natural" varies from person to person. There is no one "right" way to pattern the day.
3. **We like to graze.** Rather than taking our nourishment in two or three major infusions, called "meals," we tend to eat smaller amounts several times a "day."
4. **Sleep, too, comes in shorter segments.** Rather than one large block of sleeping and one larger block of waking in every 24-hour cycle, people sleep for shorter periods, more often.
5. **The cycle isn't 24 hours long.** Folks have their own built-in "day," and most of these natural cycles are a bit longer than 24 hours.
6. **During each cycle, we have regular ups and downs.** As anyone who has semi-slumbered through a meeting or movie well knows, not all states of wakefulness are created equal. Sometimes we're a lot more awake than at other times.

Attentiveness tends to undulate between peaks and troughs, and folks seem to hit two peaks and two troughs during each "daily" cycle.

SO, WHAT CAN YOU DO ABOUT IT?

I don't know about you, but I find this sort of information as frustrating as it is fascinating. Such findings seem to indicate that we're all living "wrong," in defiance of our own natural rhythms. Not much from this "natural" cycle seems applicable to the world of work and family and to the pattern set by clocks and calendars.

Let's take a second look. Perhaps we can make some adjustments, even while having to adhere to the basic outlines of the 24-hour day and the five-day work cycle. Here are a few ways we can acknowledge, honor, and accommodate our natural rhythms.

HOW TO FIND YOUR RHYTHM

Your body has an inherent natural rhythm. To the extent that you can, you must rediscover your rhythms and live by them. Relearn how to listen to your body and recognize when you're tired or hungry or angry or restless, rather than override these feelings because they're "improper" or simply inconvenient.

We've all picked up opinions about diet and sleep, based on experience and inclination, study, folklore, and social pressure. Sometimes these four sources agree: you love apples, science says apples are good for you, and folklore teaches, "An apple a day keeps the doctor away." And aside from the scare over the pesticides, society seems to approve of apple eating. The only real drawback seems to be that Adam and Eve business, but even there, it's the serpent, not the apple, that does the damage.

Often, though, the four influences are in conflict. "Eat your spinach," your Mama and Popeye the Sailor told you. Scientists agree that spinach is wonderful stuff. But society has singled out spinach as the very symbol of something that's good for you but is really yucky, and, truth be told, you really don't like spinach unless you mix it with at least equal parts sour cream.

Conversely, chocolate has gotten a bad rap (perhaps largely unjustly) for years, but lots of folks love to eat it, and some may even experience something like "chocolate addiction."

Smoking provides a more complex and troubling example. Most smokers start young, and peer pressure often plays a big part in getting started. Most beginning smokers react violently and negatively to their first few smoking experiences. From coughing to throwing up, the body does its best to repel the invasion of a foreign substance into the system.

If we persevere, though, the body learns to handle, then to enjoy, and finally to crave the smoke as we develop an addiction to nicotine. I've heard this addiction described by someone who would know as more powerful and harder to break than the physical dependency on heroin—powerful enough to keep people smoking even after they've developed emphysema or lost a lung to cancer.

Now science has established the causal link between smoking and these killer diseases to the satisfaction of most everyone except tobacco company executives. Twenty-five years ago the surgeon general slapped a warning on every pack of cigarettes.

Society has sent a mixed message. Ads for cigarettes originally touted the product as a health aid; athletes lent credence to this claim with their endorsements. As information from the medical community began to refute these notions, the appeal shifted to the cigarette as refreshment ("Take a puff. It's springtime"), social prop, status symbol, and image enhancer. (Marlboro didn't sell as a "woman's" cigarette with a red filter. As soon as they shed the red filter and started putting cowboys into the ads, sales took off.)

Most of our movie heroes smoked and, after a hiatus, many are now smoking again (including an angel, portrayed by John Travolta).

Smoking in public was for men—or fallen women—only. Then women gained "equality." ("You've come a long way, baby.") When the medical evidence against "secondhand," or "passive" smoke began to become pervasive and persuasive, many municipalities banned smoking in restaurants and public offices, and legal efforts to prevent sales of cigarettes to children intensified.

But already the pendulum is swinging back and the backlash for "smokers' rights" is being felt.

What have you decided about smoking? If you're a smoker or a recent ex-smoker, how many times a day do you have to decide? Have you decided that you don't really have a choice at all?

It's not as simple as just "doing what comes naturally." We initially repel the smoke but become hooked on it later.

It's not easy to know what's "approved" or "appropriate." "Society" says, among other things, that smoking is cool and that it will kill you.

But a combination of the body's initial reaction to smoking and a dispassionate review of the evidence on smoking and health can tell us what's right for us—even if we don't always do it.

Given the difficulties in knowing what's "right" and the inevitable clash between what our natural rhythms tell us and what socially enforced patterns dictate, you still might be able to alter your living pattern so that you're living more in harmony with your internal "music." Here are a few possibilities:

1. Establish a Fairly Regular Pattern

Many of us live by at least two different patterns, the work week pattern and the weekend pattern. We may reward ourselves with a late Friday and Saturday night, get up a lot later on Saturday and Sunday, and eat more and different things at different times.

Huge swings in pattern create constant disruption and the need for continuous readjustment. As we'll see in the next chapter on sleep, shift workers suffer the most from this sort of disruption. Bringing the weekend and the weekday a little closer together may help you find and adhere to your true rhythm.

2. Eat When You're Hungry, Not When It's Time

Many of us have learned not to trust ourselves to eat naturally. We may have so thoroughly trampled our own natural sense of hunger and satiation, we're not even sure when we're truly hungry or when we've eaten enough. But short of suffering from an eating disorder, we can recapture—and trust—a more natural sense, an internal sense, of when we want and need to eat.

3. Take Your Nourishment in Smaller Portions

Grazing, noshing, snacking—whatever you call it, most of us do it, and feel guilty about it. But research indicates that grazing is a healthier way to eat than packing it all in once, twice, or three times a day. Insulin-dependent diabetics learn to eat several small "meals" a day. Some of the rest of us should try it, too.

4. Nap

We'll explore the subject of sleep in greater detail in the next chapter. For now, suffice it to say that 15 minutes of sleep or rest when you really need it is much more beneficial than the hours of "catch-up" sleep you get—or try to get—later.

5. Schedule by the "Rhythm Method"

Honor thy peaks and valleys.

One of the ways the human race seems to divide itself is the great morning person/evening person dichotomy. Some of us naturally wake up early and alert. Others do not. Some of us hit our creative and productive stride about 10 at night and work well far into the morning—or about the time the morning people are getting up.

Corollary to the great morning person/evening person dichotomy: morning people marry evening people. This is one of life's great mysteries.

But many of us, morning person or evening person, have to produce by the clock. Though both report to work at 9:00, the morning person is already hitting a midday trough, while the evening person hasn't yet become fully conscious. The system serves no one but the timekeeper.

Some escape by working at home or by seeking a vocation that more accurately reflects their inner rhythms. (Could a morning person become a jazz musician? Could an evening person find happiness as a morning drive-time radio personality?)

Most of the rest of us learn to adjust to the clock rhythm, but we all pay for it.

You need to discover your own rhythms and then accommodate them as much as possible. Keep a "mood log" for a week or two. As frequently as you can during the day, jot down the time and how you're feeling. Track your mood and your energy level. The mathematically inclined can create a mood scale, 1 to 10. English majors and my other numerically impaired brothers and sisters may feel free to use descriptors. It matters only that the notations make sense to you later.

After a week or two, see if you can discern your patterns, your peak and trough times during the day and the week.

When you find them, follow them as much as you can. Plan the tasks that require creative thought and clear decision making for your peak times. Leave the relatively no-brainer tasks for the troughs. (You may even be able to sneak in a nap here, but more on that in the next chapter.)

When you can't control the schedule (the big staff meeting invariably arrives just as your energy leaves), compensate ahead of time with a little extra deep-breathing, a longer mini-vacation, maybe a brisk walk. Compensate, too, by being aware of the source of your reactions. (The boss's proposal may not really be as stupid as it seems; you're tired and grouchy, after all.)

Learning and honoring your internal rhythms is one more way you can live a more productive, happier, and healthier life.

Chapter 21

Are You Getting Enough Sleep?

Learn How to Get the Sleep You Need

You've probably never fallen asleep while giving a presentation to a large group of people—a horror brought on by a disorder known as narcolepsy.

But I'll bet you've nodded off while listening to one, yes? And I'll bet you've snoozed your way through more than one television program, school band concert, or movie.

You may have been reacting to an especially long, hard day. You may have been bored. But you may also be chronically sleep deprived. Should you be concerned? It depends on what else you've been sleeping through.

If you fall asleep every time you sit in one place longer than 10 minutes, you may have a problem.

If you catch yourself snapping awake just as your car is drifting across the center line and into oncoming traffic, you've definitely got a problem, a *big* problem, one that endangers you and everybody else on the road.

ARE *YOU* GETTING ENOUGH SLEEP?

How much is "enough"?

Your mother probably told you that you should get your eight hours every night, and Mom's wisdom stood up for decades. But in the 1950s doctors began suggesting that we could and should get by on less sleep. One prominent article in the *Saturday*

Evening Post, then a dominant synthesizer of American folk wisdom, suggested that only sluggards and dummies waste their time sleeping eight hours a night.

About that time the scientific study of sleep began (which makes it an extremely young science). We didn't even learn about a phenomenon known as REM (for rapid eye movement), the stage of sleep during which dreaming occurs, until about 30 years ago (a discovery that derived, by the way, from the observation that a dog's eyes move behind closed eyelids when it dreams its doggie dreams).

Sleep deprivation experiments (which must rank fairly high on the sadism scale) have clearly established that we need to sleep. Bad things happen when you keep folks awake for days at a time. But even here, the conclusions are murky, because some of the same bad things happen if you let folks sleep but deprive them of their dreams (another feat of cruelty accomplished by rousing sleepers every time they slip into the REM cycle but allowing them otherwise to get their "normal" sleep). After a few days of dreamless sleep, folks start having the dreams, or delusions, while they're awake, displaying the symptoms of schizophrenia. (In case you're getting worried—you *do* dream, although you might not remember your dreams.)

But we don't know *why* we dream. For that matter, we don't even know for sure why we need to sleep at all. There have been lots of theories, but research has failed to bear any of them out. One compellingly logical notion, for example, posits that we sleep so that our poor hyperactive brains can cool off. But now we know that the brain is actually more active while we sleep. Different centers light up, true, but the brain certainly isn't resting.

On the all-important question of how much sleep we need, experts are divided. Some side with Mom, suggesting that most of us do indeed need between seven and nine hours of sleep a night, with Mom's eight a reasonable average. But others suggest that "normal" sleep varies widely with the individual. Thomas Edison is often cited as an example of a highly creative and productive individual who thrived on three or four hours of sleep a night (although revisionist biographers have suggested that Edison took a lot of naps, and some even suggest that his alleged nocturnal habits are folklore).

So, we don't know for sure why we do it, and we don't agree on how much of it we need. What *do* we know about sleep?

THE FIVE STAGES OF SLEEP

"Early to bed and early to rise," Ben Franklin admonished us, attributing a practical benefit if not moral superiority to the early start. But there is probably no "normal" sleep pattern or "right" time for waking up and going to bed. Folks have very different "natural" cycles; some are simply more alert late at night and have a terrible time trying to fight their way out of deep sleep when the alarm clock rips the morning.

Getting up at dawn may do the early bird a lot of good, but it's not so good for the worm.

Sleep itself is not a single, clearly defined condition. Sleep is actually a series of five stages of progressively deeper sleep, including the REM/dream stage. Most people will cycle through the five stages three or four times during an eight-hour snooze. The dream stages tend to get progressively longer during the night, and dreams will sometimes continue from episode to episode.

Lots of books purport to interpret your dreams for you, but no one has satisfactorily explained how *you* can have a dream that *you* can't understand. (The "right side" of the brain shows its murky, symbolic films, sans subtitles, to the literal-minded "left side" of the brain?)

Some claim to be able to see future events in their dreams, and most of us certainly revisit—and often reshape—the past in dreams. Others claim to be able to teach you the techniques for lucid dreaming (conscious awareness of the dream state and the ability to change the "plot line").

...and the Things That Go Wrong in the Night

1. Insomnia is by far the most well known and common disorder preventing you from getting your sleep, so common, in fact, that most of us will suffer from it at one time or another.

As the name suggests, *sleep onset insomnia* involves difficulty in falling asleep, while *terminal insomnia* (which sounds a lot worse than it is) manifests in waking up too early and being unable to get back to sleep.

Temporary insomnia often accompanies the presence of unusually high stress, and generally the insomnia eases when the source of the stress ceases.

Doctors advise simply riding out temporary bouts of sleeplessness. If you can't fall asleep or get back to sleep in a reasonable amount of time ("reasonable," of course, depending on the individual), don't fight it. Get up and do something else (but not something stimulating) until you feel drowsy. Then try again.

Force yourself to get up at your normal time, even if you've been awake for long periods of time during the night. If you adjust your wake-up time to try to compensate for the lost sleep, you'll prolong the insomnia. The condition will pass, and the short-term loss of sleep won't really hurt you.

If the insomnia is prolonged or even chronic, get to a sleep disorder clinic (which are sprouting like bagel stores across the country, a sign of our stressed-out times).

Recent research at these clinics suggests, by the way, that some "chronic insomniacs" actually get a lot more sleep than they think they're getting. Some even sleep a "normal" seven or eight hours but still report having been sleepless for most of the night.

2. During episodes of sleep apnea, the sleeper stops breathing for a few seconds. Many people experience mild sleep apnea every night with no apparent ill effects. However, some sufferers have several prolonged sessions each night, often waking themselves—and their partners—with a sudden gasp. Sufferers from severe bouts of sleep apnea will feel fatigued and logy, even after a "full night's sleep," and may find themselves nodding off at inappropriate times during the day.

If you—or your sleeping partner—are concerned that you may have sleep apnea, you can monitor your sleep in your own bed with an apparatus called a Holter Monitor, which registers oxygen levels. The monitor involves nothing more invasive than a Band-Aid–like device on the tip of a finger. You may then "graduate" to a night of monitoring at a sleep disorders clinic to confirm the diagnosis.

3. Most of us also get the start reflex now and again, most often just as we fall asleep. Many report dreaming that they're falling, and when they tense, they "start" themselves awake.

Again, a little is normal, but a lot is trouble. Rare individuals get the start reflex dozens of times a night, robbing them of sleep.

4. Folks suffering from literal dream disorder actually act out their dreams. Most of us don't keep twitching and starting and otherwise thrashing around during the night because of a little switch at the top of the spine that prevents us from acting out our dreams. But in rare instances the little switch doesn't work.

Dream that you're running a fly pattern, about to grab a Brett Favre pass and glide into the end zone, and you may leap and run into the bedroom wall—or even out the door and down the stairs!

You don't want this disorder to go untreated, in yourself or your roommate.

SO, WHAT SHOULD *YOU* DO ABOUT SLEEPING?

Most of us will never suffer from apnea, excessive start reflex, or literal dream disorder, and our bouts of insomnia will be short-term and self-curing. But experts now suggest that most of us aren't getting enough sleep. One report asserts that 33 percent of the American population is chronically sleep deprived. Short-term, this makes us cranky and less efficient. It may be a hidden factor in many traffic accidents. We don't know the long-term consequences because we haven't been studying sleep long enough.

SIX STEPS FOR GETTING A GOOD NIGHT'S SLEEP

If you encounter sleeplessness in the form of onset or terminal insomnia or both, you may be able to treat yourself with one or more of these remedies.

1. Avoid Nicotine, Caffeine, and Alcohol

Nicotine is a powerful stimulant. It's also addicting, and it carries harmful tars and other impurities causally linked to lung cancer and other life-threatening diseases. You're clearly better off without it. If you can't go cold turkey, try to avoid smoking within a few hours of bedtime.

Caffeine is also a powerful and pervasive stimulant, present in coffee and cola, of course, but also in chocolate and aspirin tablets and lots of other less obvious sources. Caffeine reaches its peak effect about four hours after you ingest it, so that after-dinner coffee at eight may be hurting your sleep at midnight.

Alcohol is certainly not a stimulant. In fact, it's a powerful depressant. It just doesn't feel that way, because the first thing it depresses is our inhibition. But it still belongs on the short list of sleep disrupters. That shot at bedtime may help ease you into sleep, but alcohol blocks your descent into deep and restful sleep.

2. Take Sleeping Pills Short-Term or Not at All

Sleeping pills and tranquilizers may help you fall asleep and may in the short term help you get through stress-induced insomnia. But these drugs have some serious drawbacks.

- They don't work for everyone, and even have the opposite effect on some, causing prolonged wakefulness.
- They, too, block descent into deep sleep.
- You may build a tolerance, requiring larger doses to achieve the same effect.

- You can also become addicted to them.
- Worst case, you may wind up needing sleeping pills to sleep and stimulants to wake up, taking higher and higher doses of each in an extremely dangerous cycle.

3. Keep Regular Meal Times

Try to eat at approximately the same times each day, and avoid eating too close to bedtime. Digestion is a very active process and may interfere with your attempts to relax and fall asleep.

Nutritionists chime in with the advice that we'll process and use nutrients most efficiently by eating the big meal in the morning and then tapering off during the day and by eating several small meals rather than two or three large ones. However you refuel, regular habits will benefit healthy sleep.

4. Stick to Regular Bed and Rising Times

A regular sleep schedule—getting up and going to bed at approximately the same time each day—will help combat insomnia.

That means seven days a week. If you tend to follow one schedule during the work week but depart from it drastically for weekends, you may well have trouble falling asleep Sunday night and even more trouble dragging yourself out of bed Monday morning.

Folks who work split shifts have an incredibly high incidence of insomnia. The constant disruption is just too hard for most of us to adjust to.

5. Exercise Regularly

People who work out regularly report deeper, more satisfying sleep than their more sedentary brothers and sisters. Exercising on a regular schedule and not within three or four hours of bedtime is best for most of us.

All of this regularity may seem downright boring. But if you're having trouble sleeping, some adjustments here may enable you to solve the problem without drugs or other therapies.

But whatever you do, experts agree . . .

6. Don't Worry about It

There's nothing worse than lying awake thinking about how awful it is that you're not sleeping, how much you need that sleep, how bad you'll feel tomorrow if you don't get to sleep.

That is, of course, exactly what most of us do when we can't sleep.

Know that the occasional sleepless night is a natural reaction to life's stresses, and almost all of us will have our share along the way. If you can't sleep, examine your life for unusual sources of stress that may be causing the problem. If a specific problem or challenge is stealing your sleep, try the techniques we discussed in the last chapter to diffuse your anxiety.

If grief is causing your stress, know that both grief and stress will abate with time, and with them your sleeplessness. Again, your reaction is perfectly natural.

IF SLEEPLESSNESS PERSISTS . . .

If you're concerned that a chronic lack of sleep may be robbing you of efficiency and alertness, hurting your relationships, perhaps even endangering your long-term wellness, first get a clear idea of how much and when you're actually sleeping now. Keep a record for a couple of "typical" weeks, noting when you go to sleep and arise, any naps during the day, and problems or disruptions in your sleep. Include subjective narrative, noting your impressions of how deep and satisfying your sleep is.

Also note your consumption of nicotine, caffeine, and alcohol and when you eat and exercise, since this all affects your sleep.

Now you're ready for a chat with a sleep disorders expert, who may have some immediate suggestions for you or may suggest an overnight stay at the clinic for a thorough monitoring of your sleep.

IS IT A PROBLEM OR JUST A PATTERN?

So, are you sleeping "right"? Is your pattern "normal," even if it doesn't fit the schedule Ben Franklin laid out in *Poor Richard's Almanac?*

For years a good friend and colleague of mine went to bed at 10:30 each night, awoke between 2:00 and 3:00 in the morning, read for about an hour, and slept again until 5:45. By my calculations, he was getting about six hours and 15 minutes of sleep each night, and he certainly wasn't following any prescribed pattern.

He was also unfailingly alert and full of energy, a high achiever and a keen observer of life.

He may not have been "normal," but he certainly seemed to be thriving on his "abnormal" sleep pattern.

My own predilection for getting up between 4:00 and 5:00 a.m. strikes many as utterly perverse, and I used to worry about it a lot. But it seems to be natural for me. I don't use an alarm clock, and I always had a terrible time trying to "reward myself" by sleeping late on weekends. Those early morning hours are productive for me, and I truly love watching the sky lighten before the dawn.

I've stopped worrying about it. Maybe I just don't have the energy for worrying about it after years of sleep deprivation, but then again, the worrying didn't do any good, and my sleep pattern doesn't seem to be doing any harm.

How about you? Got a problem? Only you can say. If you decide that you do, this chapter has given you the tools for understanding the problem, making some life changes, or perhaps getting some help.

Chapter 22

Losing the War on Stress?

Learn How to Declare a Truce

"You know you're too stressed if you wonder if brewing is really a necessary step for the consumption of coffee."

That's part of a puckish self-examination that circulated on the Internet recently. "You know you're too stressed," the "test" continued, if

- you can achieve a "runner's high" by sitting up;
- the sun is too loud;
- you begin to explore the possibility of setting up an I.V. drip solution of espresso;
- you believe that, if you think hard enough, you can fly;
- antacid tablets become your sole source of nutrition;
- you begin to talk to yourself, then disagree about the subject, get into a nasty row about it, lose, and refuse to speak to yourself for the rest of the night;
- you find no humor in WASTING YOUR TIME reading silly "you know you're too stressed if . . ." lists.

Such satire never hits home unless it holds at least a kernel of truth.

Two social scientists named Holmes and Rahe created a more serious scale for measuring stress back in 1967. The Holmes-Rahe Social Readjustment Rating Scale assigned stress points to life situations. If you tallied 300 points or more on the scale within the last year, you were presumed to be at increased risk of illness or serious depression. Some of the events, with their point values, were:

- Death of a spouse (99)
- Divorce (91)
- Getting fired (83)
- Marital separation (72)
- Jail term (72)
- Personal injury or illness (68)
- Death of a close friend (68)
- Sex difficulties (53)
- Trouble with boss (45)
- Trouble with in-laws (43)

No big surprises here—but some serious omissions, according to sociologist Georgia Witkin. In 1991 she added new elements to the stress scale to more accurately reflect modern life in general and the evolving role of women specifically. Witkin's scale includes:

- Raising a disabled child (97)
- Single parenting (96)
- Depression (89)
- Abortion (89)
- Child's illness (87)
- Infertility (87)
- Crime victimization (84)
- Parenting parents (81)
- Raising teenagers (80)
- Chemical dependency (80)
- Son or daughter returning home (61)
- Commuting (57)

Great deal, huh? Stress depresses you, and then depression increases your stress.

Perhaps the only major surprise here is that "raising teenagers" only rates an 80. (800 seems more accurate, at least on the bad days.)

How about you? Can you tally 300 points or more, based on life events of the past 12 months? If you can, can it really make you sick?

THE PARABLE OF THE MICE IN THE REFRIGERATOR

Hans Selye is the founder of modern stress research. In one of his most famous experiments, he introduced mice to a stressful environment (in this case, the cold of a refrigerator) to see how they would react. Invariably, they went through three distinct stages. First, they fell into a funk, hunkering down to gut out a particularly long winter. (I went through a similar reaction during my first winter in Wisconsin.) But when the winter persisted, the mice went into a productive and cooperative frenzy, making nests and otherwise adapting their environment to make it more hospitable. (That's me, too, learning to put up storm windows and dressing in layers.)

Stage three really got Selye's attention and deserves ours. Almost without exception, the mice dropped dead. The cold wasn't lethal, but something about living under extreme stress for prolonged periods of time apparently was.

Subsequent researchers like Christopher Coe have made the connection. Coe separates baby monkeys from their mothers and measures the effect of this trauma on their white blood cell count. Take the monkeys from their mamas, and the white blood cell count plummets, thus depressing the immune system and leaving the monkeys vulnerable to all sorts of diseases. Reunite them, and the blood count rises.

THE FUN STUFF IS ALSO STRESSFUL

Another look at the Holmes-Rahe stress scale begins to bring the problem of stress into even sharper focus. Other items on the scale include:

- Marriage (85)
- Pregnancy (78)
- Retirement (68)
- Christmas (56)
- Addition of new family member (51)
- Vacation (43)

Wait a minute! Aren't these supposed to be the GOOD things of life, the events we work toward and wait for?

They are, but they're also very stressful, making huge demands of time and energy and requiring major adjustments.

Take Christmas. (Henny Youngman fans will no doubt add "Please.") All those preparations, the staggering expectations, the relentless requirement that you be happy! Most of us simply add this huge load to our everyday cares and responsibilities; life and work go on, Christmas or no. And just on the off chance that things don't go perfectly, you can add feelings of guilt, inadequacy, and remorse to the list of burdens.

Happy holidays!

But what about vacation—that oasis of rest and relief we struggle toward all year long?

You take on additional roles as travel agent, tour guide, recreation director, and master sergeant in charge of logistics. You exhaust yourself preparing for the trip while also trying to catch up and get ahead on your regular work. You leave familiar routines and surroundings behind for the unknown. So you're already hitting the top of the stress scale even before the first flat tire, missed plane connection, or botched motel reservation.

Are we there yet?

THE BOZO FACTOR

The world is full of bozos, and you're one of them. Don't get offended. I'm another one. We can't help it. We just keep getting in each other's way.

Put us into cars and we become particularly caustic. The guy who cuts you off in traffic stresses you. When you honk your horn at the offender, you stress the driver next to you.

Holidays, with their own sets of stressors, compound the highway insanity. "Driving probably will become even wilder now that Christmas (in P. G. Wodehouse's words) has us by the throat," George Will noted in a call for civility in the *Washington Post*. "Holidays and homicide go together like eggnog and nutmeg, so 'tis the season to study the wildness in the streets."

Relationship—or lack of relationship—inherently causes stress. Divorce is stressful (91 on the scale), but so are marriage (85), marital reconciliation (57), remarriage (worth 89 big ones on Witkin's revised scale), and—are you ready for this?—something Witkin calls "singlehood" (77).

Son or daughter leaves home and you get 41 nicks to the parental psyche. But according to Witkin, you get 61 points if your little darling moves back in.

You can't win. Enter into a relationship with another human being, get out of one, or avoid relationship all together—you open yourself to increased stress no matter what you do or don't do.

List a few of the everyday things that people do to bother you, things like

- cutting you off in traffic,
- emptying their car ashtrays in the parking lot,
- butting in line at the market,
- trying to buy more than 12 items in the 12-items-or-less line,
- talking loudly during the movie,
- chewing with their mouths open,
  and on and on.

Petty stuff? Probably. But still annoying and stressful—and unavoidable.

STRESS HAPPENS

One more plunge into the stress scale to pick up another insight into stress:

- Change of financial status (61)
- Spouse begins or ends work (58)
- Change of line of work (51)
- Change in residence (47)
- Change in number of arguments with spouse (46)
- Change in eating habits (29)
- Change in sleeping habits (27)
- Change in recreation (26)

Lose your job or get evicted from your apartment? Highly stressful. But so is winning the lottery or moving into your dream home. The one constant here is change—*regardless of the nature of the change*. All change is stressful.

Which means, of course, that living is inherently stressful. Stress is inevitable.

You can't even buy your way out of stress. Psychologist Ed Diener's recent study indicates that higher personal incomes often bring their own set of stresses.

Little wonder, then, that a recent *U.S. News & World Report* cover story announced, "Stressed Out? You've got lots of company. But there are ways to fight back."

BEING BLESSEDLY STRESSED

You can't avoid stress. But you don't really want to.

Selye and researchers who followed him have learned that the total absence of stress is no better for you than too much stress. To remove all stress from your life, you would have to remove all relationship and all challenge. That probably explains why retirement rates so high on the stress scale. Yes, you shed the responsibilities and deadlines, but you also lose definition, purpose, a reason to get out of bed in the morning.

Selye coined the term "eustress" to signify the ideal compromise—not too little, not too much, but just the right amount of stress in your life.

Your goal, then, should be to live in "eustress" as much as possible and to take especially good care of yourself during those inevitable times when you must exceed your safe stress limits.

But you may not be able to engage in safe stress by "fighting back," as that *U.S. News & World Report* headline suggests you do.

THREE GREAT LIES OF OUR AGE

We've declared war on stress. Time management is one of the weapons in our arsenal. Our battle cries include:

You can do more with less
Work smarter not harder
A leaner workforce is a more efficient workforce
(thus the terms "downsizing" and "rightsizing")

You can put these bromides on the list of "Great Lies of Our Time" (right alongside "The check is in the mail," "I'll still respect you in the morning," and "I'm not selling anything. This is an educational survey").

You *can't* do more with less. You can only do more with more. If you're working more, you're doing something else (like sleeping and playing) less.

When someone advises you to "work smarter not harder," they're telling you to produce more. They don't care if you have to work smarter *and* harder to do it.

A leaner workforce means somebody has to take on the work that somebody else was doing. If you've still got your job, that somebody is you.

Fight, manage, plan—do whatever you can to try to squeeze more work into the same limited minutes in the day—at your own risk. You're probably incurring still more stress.

So, if stress is an inevitable by-product of living, and if modern life puts us under ever greater stress, how can you possibly avoid taking on too much of it?

You probably can't, but you can *manage* the stress by understanding its nature.

THE FUNDAMENTAL TRUTH ABOUT STRESS

Stress isn't "out there" someplace, in the evil boss or the colicky kid or the traffic jam. Those are the stressors that trigger the stress.

Stress is inside you, your psychological responses to life's challenges.

Do what you can to mitigate the stressors, yes, but there's a lot you can't do anything about. You *can* do a great deal to modulate and modify your internal reactions, thus eliminating much of the stress if not the stressors.

You can learn to cope with life as it is—without letting it kill you.

You Have to Incur Stress to Lose Stress

Before you begin your strategic retreat from the stress wars, one final visit to the stress scale, where, nestled between "Trouble with boss (45)" and "Trouble with in-laws (43)" we find:

Revision of personal habits (44).

That's right. Any attempt to modify your stress response is itself stressful. So you'll need to know that you'll feel increased pressure, not relief, when you begin to retrain some of your responses to stress. Don't get discouraged. This is normal and short-lived. You'll get through it, and the benefits will be more than worth the effort.

One Size Does Not Fit All

I'm going to suggest some strategies for reducing your stress level. You'll need to modify, adapt, add, and subtract depending on your specific responses to potential stressors.

Your stress response is different from anyone else's—one more element that makes you uniquely you. We have different tolerances for pain, different energy levels, different susceptibilities to and predispositions for various diseases—and different tolerances for stress. When folks like Witkin, Holmes, and Rahe assign points to various stressors, they are at best predicting the response in the "average" person—that strange being who makes $21,914 a year, has 1.782 children, and doesn't, in fact, exist.

You also have a unique perception of what is and isn't stressful. A round of golf on a Saturday morning may be relaxing for one and a frustrating endurance test for another. It doesn't depend on how good you are at golf so much as on how much you *care* how good you are. One person's party is another person's trial. Pay attention to what stresses you and then do your best to compensate.

And now, at last, without further explanation or introduction . . .

HOW *YOU* CAN REDUCE YOUR STRESS LEVELS

1. Acknowledge and Honor Your Feelings
Some feelings seem unacceptable or even dangerous. Perhaps you've learned that it's not okay to be angry at your parents, to think less than respectful thoughts about your minister, or to lust after your best friend's spouse. You can deny such feelings, but you can't stop feeling them, and the process of denial takes psychic energy and creates stress. Feel what you feel. Then figure out how you should act—or not act—on those feelings.

2. Find Safe Ways to Express Your Feelings
Present your case to your supervisor, even if you don't think doing so will change that supervisor's decision. You'll have acknowledged and validated your feeling by giving it substance. (And your supervisor might even surprise you.)

Expressing feelings doesn't always help decrease stress, however. Rather than venting your anger, screaming at another driver in a traffic jam will actual increase the anger and your internal responses to it. You end up more, not less, stressed. In that case, you're a lot better off trying the next suggestion.

3. Unplug

You don't have to blow up every time someone lights your fuse. You can snuff out the fuse instead. How? Mom had it right; it really can be as simple as counting to 10. When you feel the anger flare, don't tell yourself you're not really angry (because it isn't "nice" to get angry). Don't rant, either. Take a deep breath and count (or laugh or spout nonsense or sing or whatever works for you).

But if you do that, you'll be letting that lousy driver ahead of you get away unpunished, right? Yeah, you will. But will screaming at him really "punish" him or "teach him a lesson"? You know it won't, and that knowledge will only frustrate you more.

Remember, too, that he's not trying to stress you out. He's not paying any attention to you at all; that's what's so annoying! He's just trying to get someplace in a hurry, just as you are.

And finally, remember that you're probably being somebody else's stressor, too. When I asked a workshop full of folks to list things other people do that annoy them, one person mentioned the bozo who crunches the ice in his soft drink at the movies. As I added the comment to our list, I silently vowed never to crunch the ice in my soft drink at the movies again.

If all that doesn't help you maintain your perspective, ask yourself this:

Is it worth making myself sick over?

All that churning inside really *can* help make you sick. And you're letting it happen to you. Do you really think "teaching" that "lesson" is worth it?

Don't get mad. Don't get even. Just get on with it.

4. Fix It

Getting annoyed at the sight of a mound of cigarette butts in the parking lot ranks high on a lot of folks' lists of annoyances. A lady in one of my recent workshops had a wonderful solution. She carries a "butt removal kit"—plastic sack, whisk broom, and pan. When she comes upon a tobacco dump, she simply removes it. Instead of getting angry and frustrated, she has accomplished something tangible to make her environment a little better.

5. Create Quiet Time Alone—Every Day

This can be nothing more than those mini-vacations we talked about earlier. But you may need more—a half hour to read or listen to music or do nothing at all.

You may *need* it, but you may not feel comfortable taking it. We spend so much time surrounded by other people and by almost constant noise, that silence and isolation can be intimidating. Don't be frightened of your own good company. Alone with your thoughts, you'll get to know yourself again.

6. Plan Your Escape Routes

When you check into a motel or hotel, do you immediately figure out how you'll get out in case of fire? You'll probably never find yourself in a motel fire, but if you do, your simple precaution might save your life.

Fire can break out in everyday life, too. Figure out how you'll escape when it does.

"When the going gets tough," Dwight Eisenhower once assured us, "the tough get going." This can mean, although I'm sure Ike didn't intend this interpretation, that if the going gets unbearable, you might need to get going—out the back door for a break before reentering the fray.

Will you find the courage to say, "Can we take a five-minute break here?" If you do, I guarantee others will silently thank you for it.

7. Wallow in Successes and Pleasures

As I write these words, William Jefferson Clinton is being inaugurated for a second term as President of the United States, complete with bands, speeches, and even a home-grown poem. Such ceremony, we're told, is good for the country, at once healing and inspiring.

I hope President Clinton is letting himself enjoy his moment to the max. Tomorrow it's business as usual, with its crises and critics and chaos.

I'm not being sworn in as President. But I am almost finished writing a long chapter in a book that's important to me. I plan to reward myself with a good, warm lunch. I intend to enjoy every bite. I'll probably tell myself what a great guy I am to have finished this chapter.

Don't just check your accomplishments off the list. Acknowledge them—and the talent, energy, and determination they required. Don't just shovel in fuel. Enjoy the pleasure of the food.

8. Give Less Than 100 Percent

Giving 100 percent isn't even good enough anymore. With inflation, athletes must now give 110 percent. But nobody really has "110 percent" to give. You have limited time, limited energy, limited resources. You can't solve every problem, meet every crisis, rise to every occasion.

Some challenges don't deserve 100 percent. Save something for later.

9. Create a Third Basket

New tasks go into the "in basket." Finished work goes in the "out basket."

And some tasks should go in the "to-hell-with-it basket."

10. Do One Thing at a Time

One of the truly pernicious lessons of modern time management involves "multi-tasking," doing more than one thing at a time.

But we dilute the effectiveness of our work and rob the joy from our pleasures when we engage in multi-tasking.

We also show a fundamental lack of respect for others if we keep typing while on the phone with a friend or hide behind the newspaper when a loved one is trying to talk to us.

Talking on a car phone while driving can endanger more than a relationship. That sort of reckless multi-tasking can endanger lives—yours and others.

Watch kids at play. They are so focused, so rapt, they truly don't hear us when we call them. You had that power of concentration once. You can cultivate it now, giving full attention to everything you do. Don't try to spin 10 plates on 10 poles. Spin one plate really well.

Chapter 23

What, You Worry?

Learn How to Stop Letting Worry
Rob You of Time and Energy

Worried about managing your time well?

You're wasting your time.

Worry steals your time and energy. It disrupts your rest, damages your ability to make decisions, and robs you of the pleasure and satisfaction you should get from work and play.

When you worry, you aren't planning, working, or solving problems. Worrying never resolves anything.

Worry ignores the present to fixate on a future that never arrives.

Worrying is like paying interest on a debt. You have nothing to show for it, you still have to pay back the principal, and you have no money left for the things you need. Substitute energy and time for money and you understand what worry really costs you.

We learn to worry, and we can learn to stop. We can replace worry with action.

THREE WAYS TO WORRY

1. **A decision you must make**: a big one ("Should I stick with the security of a regular paycheck or start my own

business?") or a small one ("Should I order the double cheeseburger with fries or the salad with lo-cal dressing?")

2. **An action you must perform:** like giving a business presentation or attending a social gathering
3. **An event outside your control**: like global warming or hostilities in Bosnia

Although the worries in the third category tend to be much larger in scope, they are also less immediate and therefore take up less of the worrier's psychic energy than do more immediate concerns, like the question of what to have for lunch.

Whatever you're worried about, you must realize that worry doesn't help.

MEASURING THE WORTH OF WORRY

1. Write down something you were worried about when you were a child.
2. Write down something you were worried about in high school.
3. Write down something you were worried about a year ago.

Now ask yourself these three questions about each worry:

1. Am I still worried about this?
2. How was the situation resolved?
3. Did worry help in any way to resolve the situation?

I'm willing to bet that in each case worry did little or nothing to help. Specific action may have resolved the situation, the passage of time may have eased or erased it, or you may have simply learned to live with it.

What are you worried about right now?

10 WAYS TO GET RID OF YOUR WORRIES

1. Don't Resist or Deny the Fear

That only sends it underground, where it will fester and grow. It will return, stronger than ever, to attack you when you're most vulnerable. Face your fear. As you stop fearing the fear, it may begin to subside. If so, worry has already done its worst.

2. Name It as You Claim It

Sometimes fear comes disguised as the formless furies, vague dread or anxiety that can shake you out of a sound sleep and leave you wide awake until daybreak. Or it may take on a specific but false aspect. You may think you're worried about the coming congressional election or the sorry shape your public schools are in—laudable concerns, to be sure—when you're really worried about a mole on your neck that suddenly changed shape and turned red.

Give it a name. Write the worry down as specifically as you can. Now you can begin to deal with it effectively.

3. Consider the Consequences

Fear doesn't exist apart from you. Like stress, it's a reaction that takes place inside you. Since you created it, you can rechannel or diffuse it.

Ask: *"What's the worst that could happen to me?"*

If you eat that cheeseburger and fries, you'll consume about a week's allotment of fat, along with an enormous number of calories. This will not do you any good, and as a regular habit, it might shorten your life. On the other hand, the one meal will not kill you—and it will taste very good.

Perhaps you're worried about that presentation you're scheduled to give in two days. What, specifically, lurks under that general performance anxiety? Perhaps you're worried that you might make a mistake and, if you do, somebody might laugh at you.

Ask: *"Could I live with that?"*
You might not like it, surely, but you could certainly live with it.
Now ask: *"What are the odds?"*
Have you been in similar circumstances? If so, how did things go then? Did you make a mistake? If so, did anybody laugh?
If you're still fretting . . .

4. Push the Worry to the Max

They won't just laugh at you. The laughter will turn to jeers. They'll start throwing things at you! They'll chase you from the room and out of the building! You'll lose your job, your spouse will leave you, and you'll wind up at the homeless shelter.

Naw. That isn't really going to happen.

Now, stop worrying, which accomplishes nothing, and prepare thoroughly for that presentation.

5. Figure Out What, If Any, Action You Will Take

You've got three choices:

- You can do something now,
- You can do something later, or
- You can do nothing.

Play with possibilities. You could eat the cheeseburger and fries now and fast for the rest of the month. You could compromise—single cheeseburger, with tomatoes and onions, no fries. You could eat the salad and steal bites of your friend's burger.

Actions you might take regarding the business presentation include: hitting the Internet to gather data; practicing in front of a sympathetic audience; faking a sore throat and going home "sick"; asking someone to make the presentation for you.

You may decide to do nothing because you feel that nothing you can do will help the situation or because the costs of any action you might take outweigh the potential benefits. Deciding to do nothing is quite different from failing or refusing to decide at all. If you examine the situation and decide there's nothing you can do, you'll remove the ambiguity and thus relieve a great deal of anxiety. If you evade the decision, you'll go right on worrying.

Perhaps you're worrying about a decision you can't make yet. If you're losing sleep over tomorrow's decision, tell yourself, "I don't have to decide that now." Repeat as often as you need to.

Now tell yourself, "Whatever I decide will be fine." Tell yourself often enough and you'll begin to believe it, not because you've brainwashed yourself but because your intuition will recognize the truth of the statement. Whatever you decide really will be fine, because you'll act on it and, having acted, move on to whatever comes next.

6. Follow Through

If you've decided on immediate action, do it!

If you've decided to do something later, write down what you're going to do and *when you're going to do it*. Be specific: date, time, and place. Then be sure to keep that appointment. Otherwise, you'll soon learn to disregard anything you write down to do later.

If you've decided to do nothing, let it go.

7. Abide by Your Decision

Make each decision once. If you decide to eat the cheeseburger, enjoy the cheeseburger. If you decide on the salad, dive in. If you decide not to eat at all, savor the virtuousness of your hunger. Whatever you do, do it wholeheartedly. Resist second-guessing yourself.

Just because you've decided on future action or on no action doesn't mean the worry will go away. If it resurfaces in your conscious mind, send it packing, reminding yourself, "I've already decided that." Do this as many times as necessary.

This may not be easy. You probably have a long pattern of worrying, perhaps going back into early childhood. And you're probably receiving some benefit from all that worry. If nothing else, worry may be serving as a substitute for action or as a means of avoiding confrontations or evading decisions. Your worries may give you a sense of engagement with life, and you might feel quite lost for a while without those familiar worries. Work your way through this discomfort. You'll emerge with time and energy for doing instead of worrying.

8. Realize You Are Not Alone in Your Anxiety

You know your inner demons well, but you never see the demons others bear. You only see the composed masks we all wear in public. That fact may lead you to assume that others aren't worried. It isn't true. People worry; they just don't show it to you. Athletes call it "putting on your game face." We all do it to get along.

Other folks probably don't see *your* fears, either. They probably figure you're cool and calm—unless you choose to tell them otherwise.

I realized the truth of this observation when I spoke at a writers' conference in Pensacola, Florida. The flight from Madison to Chicago to Pensacola was hellacious—everything but the crash. I arrived with barely enough time to get to the conference before the time I was scheduled to speak. Huge crowd, unfamiliar hall, frazzled nerves from the trip—I was a real mess. It was all I could do to stand up straight and force the first words out of my mouth. Experience carried me through the presentation.

Afterwards, several people came to the podium to chat. One woman complimented my presentation, adding, "I don't know how you do it. I would have been a nervous wreck speaking to such a large group, but you were totally at ease!"

Oh, lady, I thought. You have *no* idea.

9. Act in Spite of Your Fear

Don't wait for the fear to leave you before you act. It doesn't work that way.

Courage isn't lack of fear. Courage is action despite fear. Don't pretend to yourself that you're not afraid. Let yourself experience your fear fully. Then rechannel that fear into energy and alertness.

You will begin in fear, but soon a gentle calmness will replace that fear.

10. Protect Yourself from the Worry Contagion

The more you learn about controlling and redirecting your worry, the more aware you'll become of others' fretting and stewing. You may find yourself surrounded by colleagues who sing the "ain't it awful" blues most of the time.

If so, don't buy into their negativity and their false sense of urgency. Don't try to fix the worriers' problems. Don't try to argue them out of their worrying. Remove yourself from the blather if you can and let it roll off you if you can't.

THE FIVE FACES OF WORRY

1. Worry Festering Out of Ignorance

You can't imagine anything good coming from your present situation. You can only see bad options or no options, no way out at all.

Instead of worrying, learn. Seek information. You just don't know enough yet to see your choices, and worry is preventing you from even looking.

As new information allows you to posit possible actions, resist the reflex to reject any of them. Develop as long a list of possibilities as you can. When you've assembled your list, choose the best option or choose not to act.

2. Worrying Lurking in the Future

You're worried about a problem but can't do anything about it now, leaving you with no way to dispel your anxiety.

Instead of worrying, defer. Write down the specific time when you'll take action. Then set the problem aside. Every time the worry returns, gently remind yourself that you'll handle it at the appointed time.

3. Worrying Focused on the Past

"If only I had . . ."

"How could I have . . .?"

But you didn't. Or you did. It's done or it isn't done. Either way, it's over.

Instead of worrying, release. Is there anything you can do to make the situation better now? If so, write down the action with the specific time and place you'll do it.

If there's nothing you can do, let it go. Don't wallow in regret. As fear looks to the future, remorse dwells in the past. They are the same crippling response facing in opposite directions.

4. Worry Feeding on Inertia

Action deferred can be worry compounded. The longer you put off the confrontation, the stronger your worry may become—and the harder it will be for you to overcome it.

Instead of worrying, act. Even a "mistake" is often better than doing nothing. If you can't act now, write down the action you'll take and where and when you'll take it.

Deal with it and get on with it.

5. Worry Thriving on Evasion

Decisions carry price tags. Whatever choice you make, it may cost you something. If you don't want to face those consequences, you may simply put off the decision. Your worry will rush in to fill the vacuum you create with your lack of action.

Instead of worrying, pay the price. Calculate the true cost of your decision as best you can—in time, energy, money, and damage to relationships.

When you decide on your course of action, decide also to pay the price—and then do so, promptly.

WHAT TO DO WHEN IT'S MORE THAN WORRY

The techniques we've outlined here will get you through most worries. But we need to differentiate between worry and a genuine anxiety disorder, such as obsessive-compulsive disorder or agora-phobia.

Between 1 and 2 percent of all Americans suffer panic attacks regularly, and as much as 30 percent of the population may experience at least one in a lifetime. Symptoms include dizziness and rapid heartbeat and may become debilitating.

People with obsessive-compulsive disorder receive unwanted thoughts they are unable to dispel and engage in repetitive behavior they are unable to stop. Such behaviors frequently involve cleaning (compulsive hand-washing, for example) and checking (going back dozens of times to make sure the front door is locked).

Sufferers from agoraphobia (literally "fear of the market-place") experience panic attacks in public settings. The condition may progressively worsen, until the agoraphobic can't leave the house, a specific room, even one corner of that room. Some become paralyzed for hours at a time.

These conditions stem from biochemical predispositions of the brain. Sufferers can't simply "snap out of it," and the steps outlined in this chapter won't raise anyone out of a genuine disorder.

However, a combination of medication and behavioral therapy most likely can alleviate or even eliminate symptoms. Get help if the fears get too big.

Chapter 24

When's the Last Time You Had an Idea?

Learn How to Make Time to Think

Creativity is one of the first casualties when we allow ourselves to get too busy.

You rush from appointment to appointment, challenge to challenge. The phone rings—another disaster. You run faster and faster to keep even—never mind get ahead. There's no time to plan; you simply react.

In a moment of quiet despair, you realize that you haven't had anything resembling an original idea in weeks.

Where did your creativity go?

It didn't go anyplace. You're still thinking. In fact, you couldn't stop it if you tried. Go ahead. Sit in a corner and not-think for five minutes. How about a minute? Five seconds? Can't do it, can you? Zen masters need years of practice to learn to empty the mind.

Ah, but those aren't pearls of wisdom rattling around in your poor, distracted head, you say? More like the rattling of loose change in an aluminum can?

Listen closer. Your wisdom, your intuition, your creativity are right where they've always been, just beneath the surface of conscious thought. You just haven't had time to listen.

You have almost infinite capacity for inventiveness and creativity. But when you get caught in the time trap, you leave no time for reflection or for the incubation that yields flashes of insight.

WHY YOU SHUT YOURSELF OFF FROM YOUR GOOD IDEAS

Creative breakthroughs often derive from mistakes. Those ubiquitous Post-it notes were one such "mistake," a glue that failed to adhere as firmly as intended. Velcro was another flop, the military's attempt to create a fastener that could be "unzipped" without making any noise.

Often the "genius" idea comes disguised as irrelevancy. The folks at Pringles potato chips had no luck trying to devise a better bag for their chips, one that would keep the chips fresh and prevent crumbling. They found their answer only when they expanded the search from "bag" to "container" and began looking at crazy stuff like tennis ball cans.

Invention often comes from dogged determination, as when Thomas Edison tried out over seven hundred different materials before discovering than tungsten would glow without burning up when he allowed an electric current to pass through it.

How can you afford to try out seven hundred wrong answers? Maybe the question should be: how can you afford not to?

When you're busy, you stop seeking creative breakthroughs. You don't even welcome them if they somehow manage to thrust up through the wall of conscious thought and insist on recognition. Instead, you dismiss them as interruptions. You've already finished that project and need to get on to the next one. There's no time to go back and rethink it.

But instead of rejecting, you must embrace.

WELCOMING THE AH-HA!

The history of humanity is filled with dramatic creative breakthroughs.

Archimedes discovers the displacement theory while sitting in the bathtub one day observing the level of water in the tub fall as he stands and rise as he eases himself back into the water. Kekule dreams about a snake biting its own tail and discovers the structure of the Benzine ring after failing for years to discover it in the lab. Coleridge "writes" his "Kubla Khan" in a trance. Paul Stookey insists that he was the instrument, that his beautiful composition "The Wedding Song" played him and not the other way around.

Eureka!

Such breakthroughs come from the subconscious mind, which a man named Charles Haanel called your "benevolent stranger, working on your behalf." We all get them, but we may have shut ourselves off from them. To recapture the gift of inspiration even amidst the chaos of life, you must:

1. **Listen.** Create silence and time. Calm the din. Sit still, if just for a moment each day. Let your thoughts drift without direction.

2. **Accept.** Don't reject the idea, no matter how foolish it may seem. There's just no way to selectively welcome only the "good" ideas, the ones that are going to solve your problems. If you try to cut off the "bad" ones, you lose touch with them all and choke off the creative flows. And besides, you might not be able to tell a good thought from a bad one until you've lived with it for a time.

3. **Note.** When you receive a breakthrough, note it exactly as it came. Don't try to process, shape, apply, or direct it. Let it be what it is before you make it be something else.

CREATING THE AH-HA ON DEMAND

Can you really be creative on demand? You not only can; you have to.

Creative breakthroughs don't always or even usually come as surprise nudgings from the subconscious. In your world of constant deadlines and endless to-do lists, they are more often the product of a conscious process of problem solving.

You'll never find the time for this conscious process. No one will give you that time. You're going to have to *make* the time.

Here's a five-step process for making sure your creativity time yields the results you need.

Step 1. Make a Creativity Appointment

You've got a report to write, a presentation to prepare, a problem to solve. It will require more than just effort and time. You need inspiration.

Make an appointment to meet with that inspiration and do some brainstorming. I'm serious. Get out the calendar or the day planner and mark off a couple of one-hour sessions just for thinking.

If you don't schedule the time, you won't "find" it, and the thinking you need to do just won't happen.

Schedule that appointment at least a day and preferably longer ahead of time, and plan the session to coincide with a phase of the day when you're most alert and awake. Clear the time of all interruptions.

Step 2. Tell Your Subconscious What You Want

I know of a top executive who took his staff on a working retreat to a ski resort. He held meetings with them all day Friday, and at the end of that time, he spelled out the problem to be solved at Monday morning's meeting, admonishing them to prepare thoroughly for the session. Then he turned them loose for a weekend on the slopes.

They, of course, gave the problem no conscious thought whatsoever—which is just what he figured would happen.

He knew that the problem would lodge in the subconscious of at least some of his advisors, and when the brainstorming began on Monday morning, they would surprise him—and themselves—with insights they didn't even know they had.

Such is the power of the subconscious mind.

You can bring that same power to bear on a "brainstorming session" of one. And you don't need a ski resort to do it.

Review the problem and the solution you're after. Be sure you've defined the problem clearly and specifically, but don't limit the scope of the potential solution. (You don't want a better potato chip bag; you want a way to keep chips fresh and intact.) Then put the problem out of your conscious mind. If you catch yourself brooding on it, send it back to the subconscious.

Step 3. Stay Alert

Every student of advertising has heard the story of the fellow who comes rushing into the tire store, clutching a newspaper in his hand.

"This is amazing," the fellow tells the salesperson. "Just this morning I decided to buy four new tires for my car, and here's your ad in the morning paper advertising your prices. What a coincidence."

No coincidence. The ad had been running in the paper for years. The fellow just never saw it until he needed tires, and then the ad jumped out at him.

Advertisers use this story to explain the need for frequency; if you want your ad to be effective, you have to keep running it. But it also illustrates a principle of selective perception. When your mind becomes focused on a topic, you begin to notice material relevant to that topic. A casual conversation overheard in the elevator, a remark made over lunch, a small item on the back pages of the newspaper, a report on the evening news—suddenly the world seems to be conspiring to feed you information to help you.

Along with the conscious research you may need to perform to get ready for your "meeting," stay open to information all around you that may prove helpful.

Step 4. Play with the Possibilities

It's time to think.

You've kept that appointment with yourself, keeping the calendar clear despite all the demands made on your time. You've done your best to make sure you won't be interrupted.

You sit at your computer, or you lie on a couch with a notepad and pencil, or you walk through a park with a tape recorder in hand.

All right, you tell your subconscious. *What's the answer?*

And nothing happens.

Now what? You've fought hard for this thinking time, and now you haven't got a thought.

Relax. You've got all the thoughts you need. Your subconscious isn't holding out on you. You just asked the wrong question.

Instead of seeking *the* answer, take a few minutes to try out as many answers as you can. Here are three ways to do it.

A. Play "How Many Ways?" Make a list of as many possible solutions or approaches as you can muster. Set a timer for 10 minutes, so that you don't have to worry about the passage of time, and just let fly. Don't stop. Don't edit, evaluate, or in any way censor your thoughts. If something pops into your head, capture it on your list, even if it seems ridiculous. (I should probably say *especially* if it seems ridiculous.)

Remember Edison; there are no failures in the creative process.

"If you want to have a good idea," advertising executive Alex Osborne admonished, "have lots of ideas." (Osborne also coined the term *brainstorming*, by the way.)

B. Draw a "Tornado Outline." Write your subject or goal in the center of a large sheet of paper (or a chalkboard or flip chart or billboard or whatever you're comfortable with). Free-associate key words, phrases, statistics, anecdotes, anything that seems relevant. Again, avoid censoring ideas. (This is like the bubble outline described in Chapter 14, except it's more of a free-association approach.)

When you're done, sit for a minute or so more, to see if any stray thoughts catch up to you. Then begin linking related material and numbering items, bringing order to the chaos. You now have a working outline for further work; the hardest part of the process is finished.

C. Create a grid. Return with me now to those thrilling days of yesteryear, when the resourceful masked man and his faithful Indian companion rode the range, bringing law and order to the Old West.

Fran Striker wrote a fresh script for the *Lone Ranger* radio dramas every week for years. He had great characters to work with and a durable myth of good and evil to develop each week.

But there are only *so* many pretexts for sending Tonto into town to get beat up, and only *so* many disguises for the Lone Ranger to don; after a time Striker began to run dry.

He didn't panic. Instead, he made lists—lists of weapons, lists of disguises, lists of settings, lists of bad guys, lists of all of the elements that went into his half-hour morality tales. He would then combine items from his lists, playing with combinations until he got something that seemed promising. This system kept the Lone Ranger riding for years.

This grid or matrix system works because inspiration often occurs when an idea or image from one frame of reference collides with an idea or image from a totally different context, creating something new, surprising, and original.

"Fellow dies and goes to heaven. There's St. Peter, guarding the pearly gates and eyeing him suspiciously. St. Pete checks his scroll, scowls, then squints down at the supplicant and says, 'Smoking or non-smoking.'"

One context, heaven, collides with another context, restaurant seating arrangements.

Inspiration "strikes" when the collision occurs spontaneously, which is to say without your consciously willing it to happen. But you can create the combinations consciously through the grid system.

Step 5. Stop Before You Have To

If you can't finish in one session, break while you're still in the midst of creating ideas and certain of where you're going to go next. If you wait until you're stuck or seem to have exhausted all the possibilities, you'll carry a negative impression which can grow into dread and create a difficult start-up time when you return to the project. But if you've left your work confident of your next steps, you'll come to the plan with a positive frame of mind and ready to resume immediately.

NEW AGE? NONSENSE

Lest you think this process sounds a trifle touchie-feelie, something right out of the hippie dippy 1960s, know that people like Charles Haanel were working with these methods at the turn of the century, and Dorothea Brande spelled out a similar process for writers in a book called *Becoming a Writer* in the early 1930s. This method is solid, it's time-tested, and it works.

By actually scheduling your thinking time, you'll nurture, maintain, and increase your ability to solve problems and develop new ideas creatively. As you do, you'll recapture a hyper-alertness and an openness to possibilities, not just during those scheduled sessions, but during the rest of the time as well.

Instead of trying to find time to be creative or to fit creative thinking into your hectic life, you'll find yourself living in a constant creative state.

Chapter 25

What Are You Really Living For?

Create a Values-Based Time Management Plan

"I wish I'd spent more time at the office."

History has never recorded these as anyone's last words. I'm fairly sure it never will.

"I wish I'd spent more time with my family" is a much more likely deathbed sentiment.

List the three things in life that mean the most to you. Taken together, they might be your reason for living.

Here's how Americans completed that list in a recent national survey. The number listed next to each item indicates the percentage of people surveyed who listed it among their top three priorities. (So obviously the numbers add up to more than 100%.)

Priority	Percentage
Family life	68%
Spiritual life	46%
Health	44%
Financial situation	25%
Job	23%
Romantic life	18%
Leisure time	14%
Home	11%

Got your list? Good. Now next to each of the three note the amount of time you spend on it each week.

Shocked?

If you aren't spending large chunks of time on the three elements you've listed as the most important priorities in your life, there are three possible explanations:

1. Important things don't necessarily require a lot of time.
2. You're mistaken about your priorities.
3. You aren't putting your time where your priorities are.

Let's examine each explanation.

DOES THE WAY YOU SPEND YOUR TIME TRULY REFLECT YOUR VALUES?

The Myth of "Quality Time"

Two strong social forces combined to move Harriet Nelson and June Cleaver out of the kitchen and into the workforce.

First, we began to require two salaries to keep up with our increasing material expectations. In 1985, less than 2 percent of American homes had CD players in them, and only about 7 percent had answering machines. By 1996, two thirds of our homes had CD players and 63 percent had answering machines. These are our new "necessities."

At the same time, women began giving public expression to the notion that being "just" a housewife didn't allow them to develop fully or to take their place as equal partners with men in society. They didn't just need jobs; they wanted careers.

As more and more former stay-at-home moms took jobs outside the home, the myth of the Superwoman developed. "You can have it all" translated into "You must DO it all!"

Surveys noted that the distribution of housework didn't change in many homes even when the woman took an outside job. After a full day's work at the office, many women came home to another full day's work.

The term *quality time* was born.

As women joined their husbands in having less and less time for the kids and for their partners, social thinkers (i.e., freelance magazine writers) developed the theory that a little bit of very good time together would compensate for the lack of lots of time together. The more we talked about "quality time," the more we came to believe in its reality.

But "quality time" is a sham, a hoax, a cruel delusion. Instead of "quality time," we simply have less time, and what time we've got is really "pressure time."

If you can honestly tell me that you can schedule a meaningful conversation with your adolescent son or daughter, or that lovemaking by appointment doesn't lose a little something in spontaneity, I'll believe in "quality time." But relationships don't work that way. You can no more force a teenager to talk before he or she is ready than you can convince a cat to play Scrabble.

There's no hurrying or scheduling meaningful moments, breakthrough conversations, wonderful gestures. They occur in the midst of the muck, often when we least expect them. If you aren't spending time with a loved one, you're going to miss many of those moments. And you'll be putting much too heavy a burden on the time you do have together. "Quality time" turns into tension time.

ARE YOU MISTAKEN ABOUT YOUR PRIORITIES?

If you aren't spending much time on family or spiritual life or health maintenance, for example, then maybe these aren't really the most important things in your life.

Could you be wrong about your own priorities? Well, sure. In the incredibly complex interactions of conscious mind, subconscious motive, and psyche, we're perfectly capable of masking our true motivations from ourselves even as we might seek to hide them from or misrepresent them to others.

Also, the process of writing a list of priorities is different from the process of living your life. Your list could reflect the things you think of when asked to make a list, just as the opinion you give to a pollster might represent the opinion you would have if you had an opinion.

You might have listed the elements you think you're *supposed* to list, the elements it's acceptable or right to value most highly. You really wanted to list "making a pot of money" as your number-one priority, but somehow you just didn't feel right doing so. You knew that "family" was the "right" answer.

It's possible that you misrepresented your priorities—on a list that only you will see, in a book designed solely to help you make decisions about how you spend your time. It's possible—but it isn't very likely.

If you'd like to go back now and change your list to accurately reflect your values, that's ok. It's your list. But I suspect you got it right the first time.

Which brings us to the third possible explanation, that you aren't putting your time where your heart is.

WHY AREN'T YOU SPENDING TIME ON THE IMPORTANT STUFF?

Actually, there are three rather simple explanations, and none of them requires that you be a beast, a hypocrite, or a fool.

1. Time Spent Making Money Is Time Spent on the Family

We aren't just working for VCRs and second cars. We're working to feed and clothe our children and to keep a roof over our heads. We're working so that the government won't have to take care of us. We're working so that we'll be self-sufficient even when we're too old to work (or we're pushed out of our jobs because of a mandatory retirement age).

If you're lucky, your vocation may also be an avocation, even a passion, helping you to grow and develop intellectually. You may have been able to integrate your spiritual life and your work life. It isn't necessarily a strict either/or choice.

2. Working at Your Job Is Easier Than "Working at" Your Family

Jobs often comprise well-defined tasks. They aren't necessarily easy or even pleasant, but they're clear. You know what you're supposed to do, and you know what it's supposed to look like when you finish. Something outside yourself tells you when you've done well and when you need to work harder.

Knowing exactly how to "have a good family life" or to "be healthy" can be a lot harder, and the "product" of your efforts here is often intangible.

3. Social Pressure Rewards Traditional Concepts of Work

Even when you begin telling yourself that other aspects of life are important, too, you don't slack off on the job expectations in the slightest. Somehow you're supposed to devote more time to family without taking a minute from work—more of that "you can do more with less" nonsense, the underpinning for a belief in "quality time."

HOW TO LIVE A VALUES-CENTERED LIFE

You aren't a monster or even a hypocrite. You're simply a time-pressured American without enough hours in your day for the important things in life. That explains it, but it doesn't fix it.

What can you do to make or find or create time for family, for spiritual growth, for health maintenance?

"There's right and there's wrong," John Wayne as Davy Crockett told us in *The Alamo*. "You gotta do one or the other. You do the one, and you're living. You do the other, and you may be walking around, but you're dead as a beaver hat."

If only life were that simple. But to do the right thing, you have to know the right thing to do.

Knowing the right thing to do, then, must dwell at the core of any real time management program.

Your values, your definition of the right way to live, are inside you. It's time to get them out so that you can live by them.

Step 1. Create a Personal Mission Statement

Most businesses and organizations have one—although the employees and members may be unaware of it. The mission statement is much more than policies and procedures governing day-to-day activities (though daily activities should reflect and contribute to the mission). The mission statement describes what the organization wants to be and what it wants to accomplish. Ideally, every member of that organization should contribute to building the statement and then should work to embody it.

What's your mission in life? Why are you living? What do you hope to be and do with your life? What values and assumptions underlie your core mission?

Spend some time with these questions. Let them dwell in your subconscious. Come back to them again and again. Be ready always to change and renew your answers as you grow in experience and wisdom.

Then you're ready to move on to a critical second set of questions:

- How will you act on what you believe?
- How will your life reflect your values?
- How can you live to fulfill your mission?

Step 2. Define Values in Terms of Actions

Let's suppose that, like two thirds of all Americans polled, you listed "family life" as among your top three priorities in life.

What actions can you take—and what actions will you avoid—to live out that value?

My father once turned down a chance to take a new job for more money because the new job would have required a great deal of travel. "I wanted to be home at night to hear your prayers," he explained to me much later.

For my father, raising his sons translated into being there to tuck us in at night. It also meant checking our math homework, coaching a Little League team, serving as an adult Boy Scout leader, taking us fishing and to ball games, and lots of other activities, all of which took time and commitment. I know he enjoyed doing these things with us, but I also know now how tired he must have been sometimes, how much he might have longed to sit on the porch with his feet up instead of going out and hitting fungoes for his son the would-be center fielder.

Core values translated into daily doing. My father lived his commitment.

What does a commitment to "spiritual life" mean in terms of activities? It could mean going to church weekly (or monthly, or sometimes), reading and reflecting, participating in a prayer group, going on a week-long silent retreat. What does it mean to you? When you answer this question, you have created the possibility that you can live out this value in your life.

Step 3. Schedule for Your Values

If you don't get it on the schedule, it isn't going to happen.

That's the difference between a New Year's Resolution to "lose 10 pounds" and a Monday–Wednesday–Friday 7 a.m. appointment to take an aerobics class at the local Y.

Put it on the day planner. Be as conscientious about keeping that appointment as you would about an audience with the president or a quarterly evaluation with the boss.

Step 4. Go Gently into That New Life

Conscientious, yes. Firm in resolve and consistent in action, you bet! But judgmental and unforgiving, never!

As you seek to change the way you live, remember one of the lessons we learned at the beginning of this journey: *all change, including changes in personal habits, is stressful.*

Old habits are hard to break, and daily life patterns are the most deeply ingrained habits of all. (To illustrate this truth for yourself, simply try putting on your pants "wrong leg" first.) You're going to forget, and you're going to slip back into old ways.

You're also going to be overpowered by life at times, no matter how carefully you've planned and how well you've anticipated.

Don't berate yourself. Gently remind yourself and do differently next time. Slowly the new way will become the "right" way, the "natural" way.

Give yourself credit for what you do; don't just blame yourself for what you fail to do. If you finish 15 of the 17 items on that to-do list, rejoice in what you've done. Those other two items are what tomorrow was invented for.

Do one thing at a time, with all your energy, your attention, your heart.

And finally, with all the planning and evaluating and scheduling—*don't try to do too much.*

Time management isn't about maximizing the number of items you can check off in a day or a life. It's about living fully, productively, joyfully—by your definitions of these terms.

I'll end this with these words of philosopher/theologian Thomas Merton:

The rush and the pressure of modern life are a form,
perhaps the most common form,
of its innate violence.
To allow oneself to be carried away by a multitude of
conflicting concerns,
to surrender to many demands,
to commit oneself to many projects,
to want to help in everything
is to succumb to violence.
The frenzy of the activist neutralizes work for peace.
It destroys the fruitfulness of work,
because it kills the root of inner wisdom
which makes work fruitful.

Index

A

Adrenaline rush, 4-5
Agendas, for meetings, 85
"Age of Leisure," 6-7, 104
Agoraphobia, 205
"Ah-ha!" experience, making time for, 207-214
Alcohol, and sleep, 178
"Annoyance factor," and technology, 101
Anxiety disorders, 204-205
Associated Press Style Book, 123

B

Biorhythms, 165-172
and exercise schedule, 57
Blocks, motivational, 37, 40, 154-155
Brainstorming, 212
Breaks
as stress reduction, 193
taking before needed, 41, 121-122, 213-214
during tasks, 45-48
in to-do lists, 34-35
during waiting times, 146
Breathing, as relaxation, 45-46
Bubble outlines, 120-121, 212
"Busy work," 81, 159-160

C

Caffeine, 178
Calendars
and exercise schedule, 57
leaving blank space in, 75-76
management of, 76-77
and scheduling meetings, 74-75, 138
Cellular phones, 97
Change, stress of, 186-188
Choices
about extra commitments, 87-96
about technology selection, 98-99, 106
and "got a minute?" question, 72-78
personal control over, 59-69
Christmas, stress of, 186-187
Cigarettes, 168-170, 178
Clocks, dependency on, 2-4
Clothing, decisions regarding, 60
Clutter, 131-139. *See also* Desk/workspace, organization of; Filing; Paper flow, control of
reasons/rationalizations for, 133-135
Coe, Christopher, and stress research, 185
Commitments, extra
motives for, 88-90
saying no to, 87-96
true cost of, 90-91
Commitment, to project, and procrastination, 150-151
"Communication-free zones," creation of, 107, 124
Communications
face-to-face, vs. e-mail, 103
prioritizing of, 107

"Compost heap" file, for
    paperwork, 129
Control
    of paper flow, 125-129
    personal
        and "got a minute?" question,
            72-78
        over extra commitments, 87-96
        over time management,
            20-21, 23-24, 59-69
    and technology, 105-107
Cost
    of extra commitments, 90-91
    of technology, 98-101
Creativity
    making time for, 207-214
    systems for sparking, 212-213
Criticism, and work projects, 40-41

D
Day planners. See Calendars
Deadlines
    and adrenaline rush, 4
    and technology, 104
Decisions
    about extra commitments, 87-96
    about technology use, 106-107
    and "got a minute?" question,
        72-78
    personal control over, 59-69
    and worrying, 197-198, 201-202
Deep breathing, as relaxation,
    45-46
Delegating, 161-162
    and desk clutter, 132-133
Desk/workspace, organization of,
    23, 126, 131-139
Diet, 55
    and biorhythms, 167-168, 170
    and sleep, 179
Direct Marketing Association, and
    mailing-list removal, 127
"Doing more with less," fallacy of,
    xvii-xviii, 7, 189-190

Downtime
    productive use of, 145-147
    and technology, 100
Dreaming, during sleep, 174-175,
    177

E
Eating. See Diet
Editing, 122-123
The Elements of Style, 123
E-mail. See also Technology
    impersonality of, 102-103
    and "last-minute syndrome,"
        104
    pros/cons of, 123-124
    time spent on, 18, 103
Emotions, and stress, 191
Evasion, worry stemming from,
    204
Exercise
    defining goal of, 56
    scheduling, 57
    and sleep, 179
Expectations
    increased by technology, 104
    and perfectionism, 164
Expendability, myth of, and extra
    commitments, 88

F
Facts vs. opinions, on Internet, 114
Family, and time management,
    218-221
Faxes. See Technology
Fear
    and procrastination, 152-153
    and worrying, 199
Feelings, and stress, 191
Filing, 128, 136-138, 157-159
Future, worrying about, 203

G
Gadgets. See Technology
Goals

breaking into steps, 55-56
long-range, on to-do lists, 35
"Got a minute?," as time-stealing
question, 71-78
Grid/matrix system, for creative
thinking, 213
Guilt, and extra commitments, 88

H
Health, and "speed sickness," 5-6
Henderson, Bill, and technology,
105
"High touch," and technology,
101-102
Holidays, stress of, 186-187
Holmes-Rahe Social Readjustment
Rating Scale, and stress
measurement, 183-186
Holter Monitor, for sleep apnea,
177
How to Put More Time in Your
Life, 23

I
Ideas, making time for, 207-214
Ignorance, worry stemming from,
203
Illness, and to-do lists, 31-32
"Important" vs. "urgent," 59-69,
82, 163
Indispensability, myth of, and extra
commitments, 88
Inertia, worry feeding on, 204
Information
from Internet, verification of,
113-115
vs. wisdom, 112
Information overload, 109-118
Insomnia, 176, 180
Internet, 18
"addiction" to, 112
fundamental truths about, 111-112
and information overload,
109-118

and information verification,
113-115
and other media, 111-112
surfing on, scheduling time
for, 118
as time-waster, 103
"I" statements, during meetings,
85-86

J
Judgment, and work projects,
40-41

K
Keyboard, composing on, 121

L
Lakein, Alan, and to-do lists, 27
"Lakein Question," 67
"Last-minute syndrome," and
technology, 104
Lateness, 143-144
Lead Pencil Society, 105
"A leaner workforce is a more
efficient workforce," fallacy of,
189-190
Learning, and new technology, 99
Leisure time
activities during, 13-14
increase in, 12
lack of, 4-7
and technology, 104
Letters. See E-mail; Mail (paper);
Paper flow, control of
Lists
not-to-do, 36, 160-161
to-do, 27-36, 68
dependency on, 35-36
misuse of, 27-29
order of items on, 33
suggestions for creating,
30-36
Literal dream disorder, 177
Log

of moods/biorhythms, 171-172
of time spent, 14-18
Long-range goals, on to-do lists, 35

M
Mail (paper), 137-139
Mailing lists, removal from, 127
Management
of calendars, 76-77
of other staff, 81-86
of paper flow, 125-129
time. *See* Time management
Matrix/grid system, for creative
thinking, 213
McGee-Cooper, Anne, and to-do
lists, 27-28
Media, and Internet, 111-112
Meetings
decreasing time spent in, 83-86
preparation for, 84-85
scheduling, 74-75, 138
Memos. *See* E-mail; Mail (paper);
Paper flow, control of
Mental preparation, for work
projects, 37-38
Mission statement, personal, 220
Mothers, working, and lack of
leisure time, 6-7, 13
Motivation
and procrastination, 150-156
and staff management, 83
Motivational "blocks," 37, 40,
154-155
Multi-tasking, 22-23
and stress, 194-195
Muscular tension, 47

N
Napping, 171. *See also* Sleep
Natural body rhythms. *See*
Biorhythms
"Newslink," on Internet, 117
News services, online, 117
Nicotine, 168-170, 178

"No"
as answer to "got a minute?," 73
and extra commitments, 87-96
how to say, 95-96
Not-to-do list, creation of, 36,
160-161

O
Obsessive-compulsive disorder,
205
Online. *See* Internet
Opinions vs. facts, on Internet, 114
Organization
of desk/workspace, 23, 126,
131-139
of paperwork, 125-129
personal style of, 51-58
Outlines, 120-121, 212

P
Panic attacks, 205
Paper flow, control of, 125-129,
157-159. *See also* Desk/
workspace, organization of;
Filing
Past, worrying over, 204
Perfectionism, 163-164
Periodicals, reduction of, 138
Personal mission statement,
creation of, 220
"Personal touch," and technology,
101-102
Physical preparation, for work
projects, 38-39
Planners. *See* Calendars
Planning, for work projects, 39
Positive visualization, 38, 46
Preparation, for work projects,
37-39
Pressure, working under, and
adrenaline rush, 4
Prioritizing
of communications, 107
and procrastination, 153-154

and significant others, 77
using "want/need" question,
    67-68
of values, 215-222
Procrastination, 149-156
and technology, 104
Projects
    breaking into smaller parts,
        33-34, 55-56
    delegating/swapping of,
        160-162
    jump-starting, 37-41
    and procrastination, 150-156
    stopping before necessary, 41,
        121-122, 213-214
Pushcart Press, 105

Q
"Quality time," myth of, 216-217

R
Rapid-eye-movement sleep,
    174-175
Reading
    and leisure time, 13
    and paper flow management,
        128-129
    during waiting times, 116
Relationships. See also Family,
    and time management
    and prioritizing, 77
    stress of, 187
Relaxation
    as stress reduction, 193
    taking before needed, 41,
        121-122, 213-214
    during tasks, 45-48
    in to-do lists, 34-35
    during waiting times, 146
REM sleep, 174-175
Repairs, and technology, 100
Responses, to paperwork, 127-128,
    138
Rest

as stress reduction, 193
    taking before needed, 41,
        121-122, 213-214
    during tasks, 45-48
    in to-do lists, 34-35
    during waiting times, 146
Rhythms of body. See Biorhythms
Robinson, John, and increased
    leisure time, 12

S
Saying "no"
    to extra commitments, 87-96
    to "got a minute?," 73
    how to, 95-96
Scanning, and Internet
    information, 115-116
Schedule/scheduling
    for creativity "appointments,"
        210
    for exercising, 57
    leaving blank spaces in, 75-76
    for mail responses, 138
    for meetings, 74-75
    and sleep, 179
    for values/priorities, 221
Scott, Dru, on clutter, 23
Selection, of technology, 98-99
Selective perception, and creativity
    breakthroughs, 211
Selye, Hans, and stress research,
    185
Shor, Juliet, and increased work
    hours, 11
Shoulder tension, 47
Sickness. See also "Speed
    sickness"
    and to-do lists, 31-32
Skimming, and Internet
    information, 115-116
Sleep, 22, 173-181
    and biorhythms, 165, 167-168,
        171
    disorders of, 176-177

stages of, 174-175
tips for getting, 178-180
tracking of, 14-16
Sleep apnea, 176-177
Sleep deprivation, 177-178
Sleeping pills, 178-179
Sleeplessness. *See* Insomnia; Sleep
Smoking, 168-170, 178
Sources, on Internet
  bookmarking, 116-118
  verification of, 113-114
"Speed sickness," 1-9
  symptoms/consequences of, 5-6
Speed writing, 119-124
Spiritual life, and time
  management, 221
Staff, management of, 81-86
Start reflex, during sleep, 177
Start-up rituals, and work projects,
  37
Steps
  breaking goals into, 55-56
  in reducing clutter, 135-137
  unnecessary, elimination of,
    157-159
Stress, 183-195
  coping with, 190-195
  inevitability of, 188
  measurement of, 183-186, 188
  as psychological response,
    190-191
Subconscious mind
  and creative breakthroughs,
    208-211
  and mental preparation, 37-38
"Surfing" Internet, scheduling time
  for, 118
Swapping work projects, 162
"Switchboard," on Internet, 117

T
Tardiness, 143-144
Technology
  and increased expectations, 104

and information overload,
  109-118
and personal control, 105-107
and "personal touch," 101-102
and staff management, 81-82
and time management, 97-107
as time-waster, 103
true cost of, 98-101
Telephones, 97
  decision to answer, 61-63
Television, 12-13
Tension
  muscular, 47
  and two-minute breaks, 45-48
The Overworked American, 11
Time
  definitions of, 8-9
  estimation of, 2-4
  "finding/saving," fallacy of,
    68-69, 103-105
  leisure. *See* Leisure time
  tracking of (time log), 14-18
  unstructured, fear of, 7
  wasters/eroders of, 71-79
Time management
  and new technologies, 97-107
  as social issue, 19-20
  traditional, limits to, 21-24
  values-based, 215-222
Time Management for
  Unmanageable People, 27-28
Time Management: How to Get
  Control of Your Time and Your
  Life, 27
Time-savers. *See* Technology
To-do lists, 27-36, 68
  dependency on, 35-36
  misuse of, 27-29
  vs. *not*-to-do lists, 36, 160-161
  order of items on, 33
  suggestions for creating, 30-36
Tornado outlines, 212
"Touch it once" rule of paper
  management, 126, 138-139

Touch-typing, 121
Tranquilizers, 178-179
Two-minute breaks, during work, 45-48

U
Unnecessary steps, elimination of, 157-159
Unstructured time, fear of, 7
"Urgent" vs. "important," 59-69, 82, 163

V
Vacations, stress of, 186
Values, and time management plans, 215-222
Verification, of Internet information, 113-115
Visualization, 38, 46
Voice mail, 97-98
Volunteering
   for extra commitments, 87-96
   motives for, 88-90
   true cost of, 90-91

W
Waiting, 141-147
   inevitability of, 144-146
   productive use of, 145-147
   reading file for, 116
"Want/need" question, and prioritizing, 67-68
Wasters, of time, 71-79
Watches, dependency on, 2-4
Witkin, Georgia, and stress measurement, 184

Women, and lack of leisure time, 6-7, 13
Work aversion, 37. *See also* Procrastination
"Work avoidance" work, 159-160
Working hours, increase in, 11
Working mothers, and lack of leisure time, 6-7, 13
Work projects
   breaking into smaller parts, 33-34
   delegating/swapping of, 162
   jump-starting, 37-41
   and procrastination, 150-156
   stopping before necessary, 41, 121-122, 213-214
"Work smarter, not harder," fallacy of, 7, 189-190
Workspace. *See* Desk/workspace, organization of
Worry, 197-205
   about sleep, 180
   getting rid of, 199-203
   measuring worth of, 198
   and to-do lists, 32
   types of, 203-204
"Writer's block," 37, 40, 154-155
Writing
   and editing, 122-123
   tips for, 119-124

Y
"You can do more with less," fallacy of, xvii-xviii, 7, 189-190

Marketing Magic
Don Debelak

Marketing Magic provides the action-oriented strategies that help you attract new customers and keep the ones you have.
$9.95, 1-55850-704-3

Selling 101
Michael T. McGaulley

Selling 101 provides the key sales techniques you need to build your sales, whether you're selling a product or a service, whether you have any previous sales experience or not.
$9.95, ISBN: 1-55850-705-1

Service, Service, Service
Steven Albrecht

Service management authority Steven Albrecht shows how to develop the high quality service programs that keep customers coming and leaves the competition in the dust.
$9.95, ISBN: 1-55850-758-2

Available Wherever Books Are Sold

If you cannot find these titles at your favorite retail outlet, you may order them directly from the publisher. BY PHONE: Call 1-800-872-5627. We accept Visa, Mastercard, and American Express. $4.95 will be added to your total order for shipping and handling. BY MAIL: Write out the full titles of the books you'd like to order and send payment, including $4.95 for shipping and handling, to: Adams Media Corporation, 260 Center Street, Holbrook, MA 02343. 30-day money-back guarantee.

Find more on this topic by visiting BusinessTown.com

Developed by Adams Media, **BusinessTown.com** is a free informational site for entrepreneurs, small business owners, and operators. It provides a comprehensive guide for planning, starting, growing, and managing a small business.

Visitors may access hundreds of articles addressing dozens of business topics, participate in forums, as well as connect to additional resources around the Web. **BusinessTown.com** is easily navigated and provides assistance to small businesses and start-ups. The material covers beginning basic issues as well as the more advanced topics.

✓ **Accounting**
Basic, Credit & Collections, Projections, Purchasing/Cost Control

✓ **Advertising**
Magazine, Newspaper, Radio, Television, Yellow Pages

✓ **Business Opportunities**
Ideas for New Businesses, Business for Sale, Franchises

✓ **Business Plans**
Creating Plans & Business Strategies

✓ **Finance**
Getting Money, Money Problem Solutions

✓ **Letters & Forms**
Looking Professional, Sample Letters & Forms

✓ **Getting Started**
Incorporating, Choosing a Legal Structure

✓ **Hiring & Firing**
Finding the Right People, Legal Issues

✓ **Home Business**
Home Business Ideas, Getting Started

✓ **Internet**
Getting Online, Put Your Catalog on the Web

✓ **Legal Issues**
Contracts, Copyrights, Patents, Trademarks

✓ **Managing a Small Business**
Growth, Boosting Profits, Mistakes to Avoid, Competing with the Giants

✓ **Managing People**
Communications, Compensation, Motivation, Reviews, Problem Employees

✓ **Marketing**
Direct Mail, Marketing Plans, Strategies, Publicity, Trade Shows

✓ **Office Setup**
Leasing, Equipment, Supplies

✓ **Presentations**
Know Your Audience, Good Impression

✓ **Sales**
Face to Face, Independent Reps, Telemarketing

✓ **Selling a Business**
Finding Buyers, Setting a Price, Legal Issues

✓ **Taxes**
Employee, Income, Sales, Property, Use

✓ **Time Management**
Can You Really Manage Time?

✓ **Travel & Maps**
Making Business Travel Fun

✓ **Valuing a Business**
Simple Valuation Guidelines

http://www.businesstown.com